Songs of Peace, Hope & Love

ISBN 978-1-4803-4430-3

HAL•LEONARD®
CORPORATION

7777 W. BLUEMOUND RD. P.O. BOX 13819 MILWAUKEE, WI 53213

For all works contained herein:
Unauthorized copying, arranging, adapting, recording, Internet posting, public performance,
or other distribution of the printed music in this publication is an infringement of copyright.
Infringers are liable under the law.

Visit Hal Leonard Online at
www.halleonard.com

ANYWAY

Words and Music by BRAD WARREN,
BRETT WARREN and MARTINA McBRIDE

Moderate Ballad

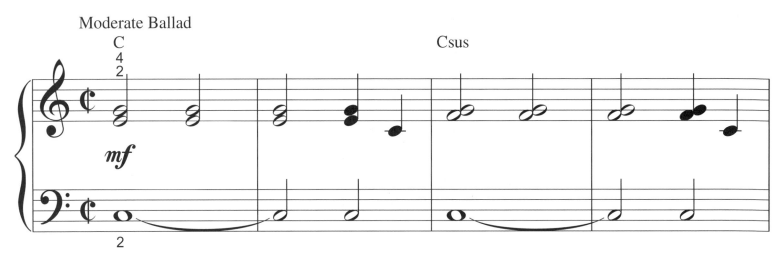

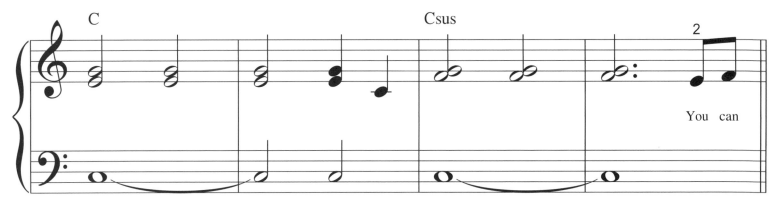

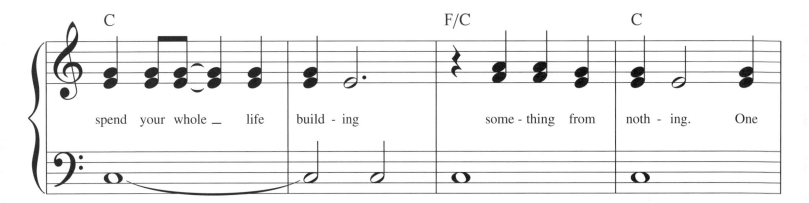

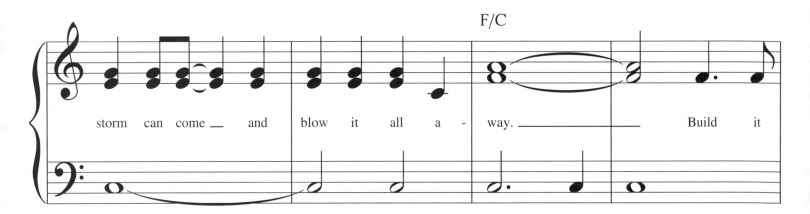

© 2011 EMI BLACKWOOD MUSIC INC., STYLESONIC MUSIC, LLC and DELEMMAVA MUSIC PUBLISHING
All Rights for STYLESONIC MUSIC, LLC Controlled and Administered by EMI BLACKWOOD MUSIC INC.
All Rights Reserved   International Copyright Secured   Used by Permission

an - y - way. ____

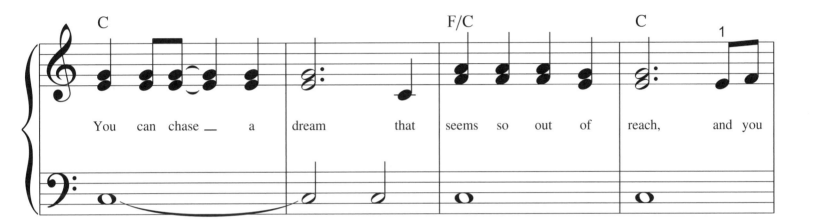

You can chase ___ a dream that seems so out of reach, and you

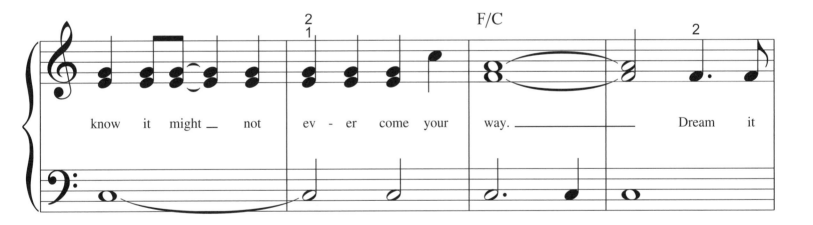

know it might ___ not ev - er come your way. ____ Dream it

an - y - way. ____

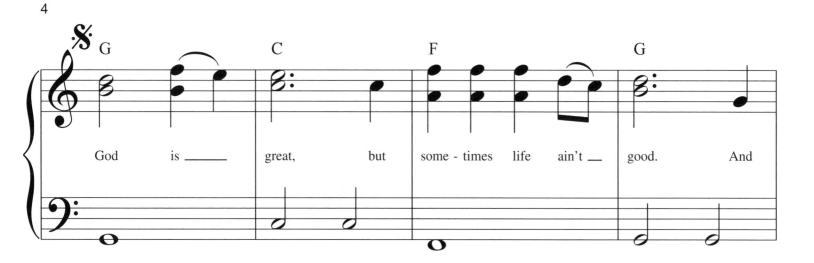

God is _____ great, but some - times life ain't _____ good. And

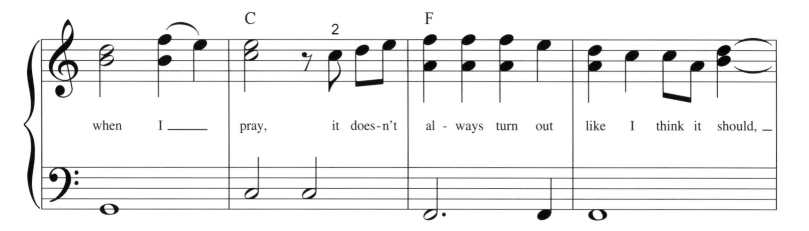

when I _____ pray, it does-n't al - ways turn out like I think it should, _____

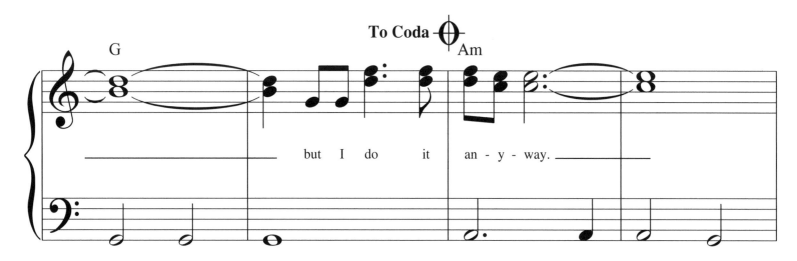

To Coda ⊕

but I do it an - y - way. _____

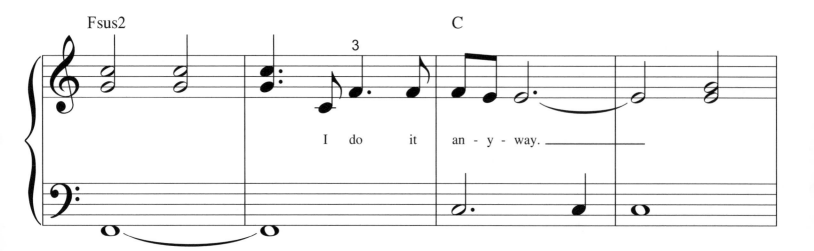

I do it an - y - way. _____

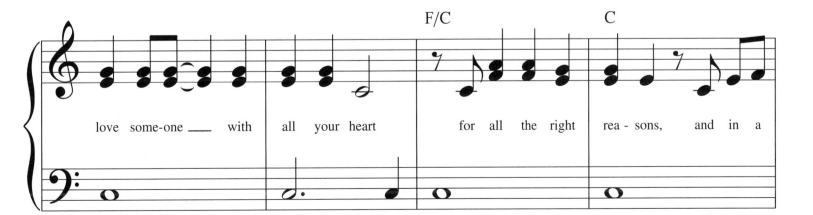

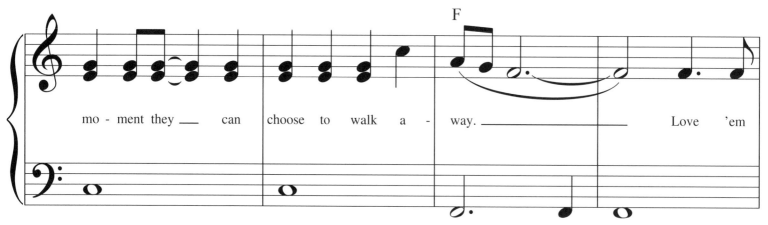

mo - ment they ___ can | choose to walk a - way. ___ Love 'em

an - y - way. _____

D.S. al Coda

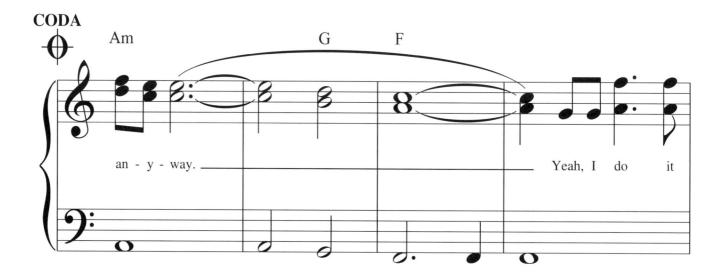

CODA
an - y - way. _____ Yeah, I do it

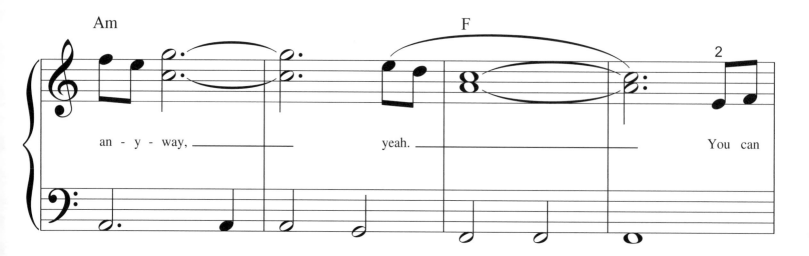

an - y - way, _____ yeah. _____ You can

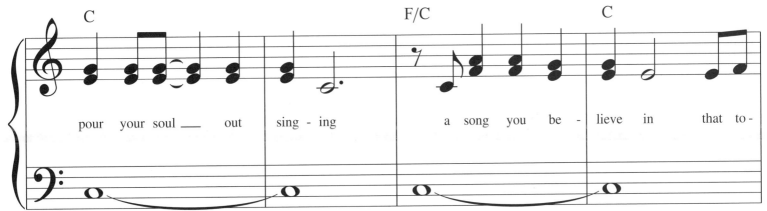

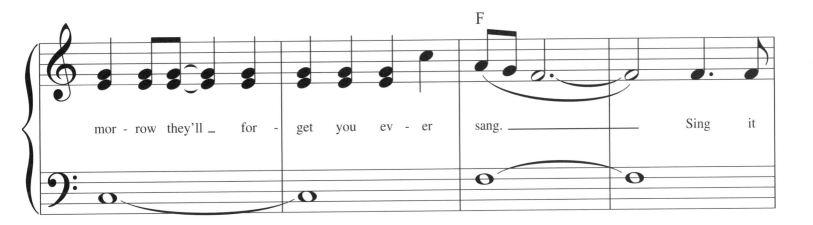

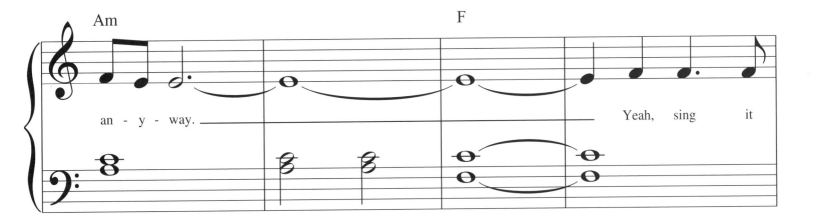

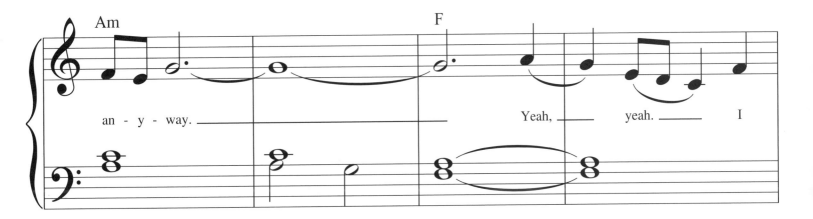

8

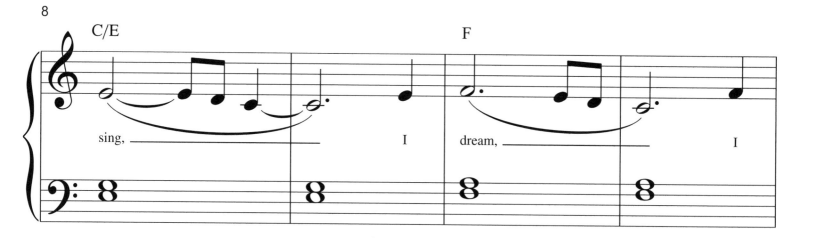

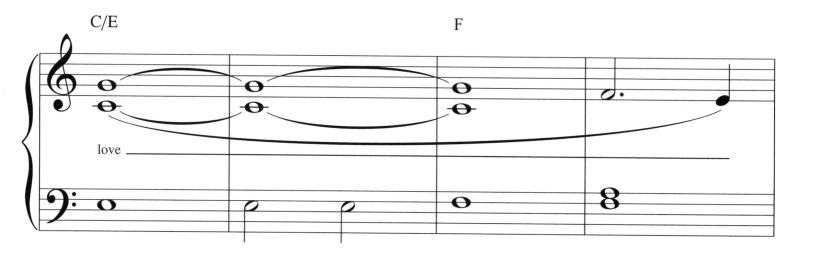

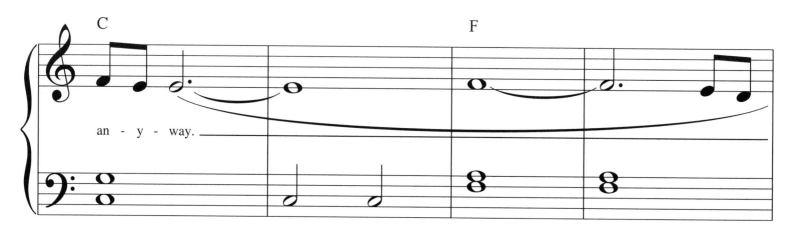

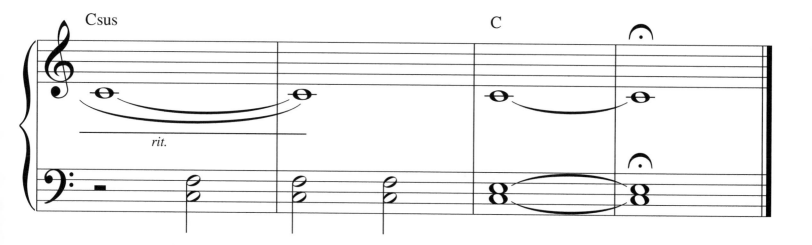

THE CLIMB

from HANNAH MONTANA: THE MOVIE

Words and Music by JESSI ALEXANDER
and JON MABE

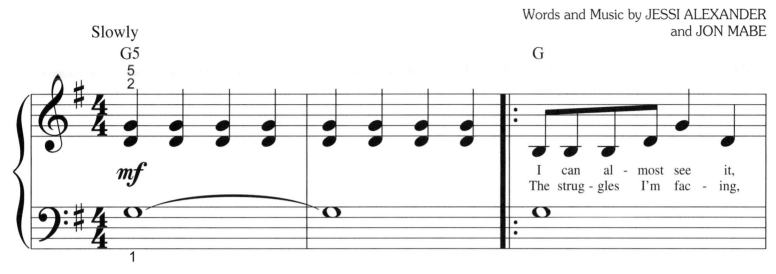

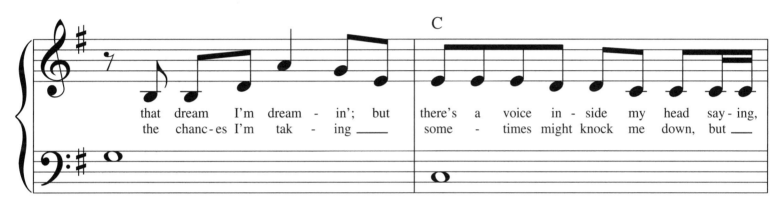

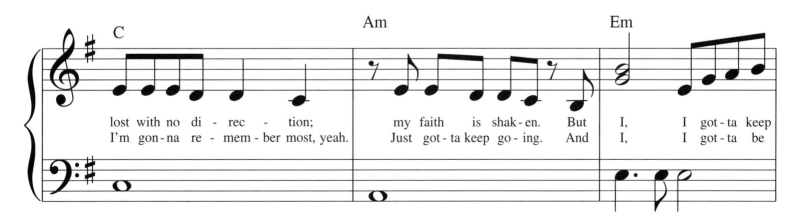

© 2007, 2009 Vistaville Music, Hopeless Rose Music, Music Of Stage Three and Mabe It Big
All Rights for Hopeless Rose Music Administered by Vistaville Music
Worldwide Rights for Music Of Stage Three and Mabe It Big Administered by Stage Three Music (US) Inc., a BMG Chrysalis company
All Rights Reserved   Used by Permission

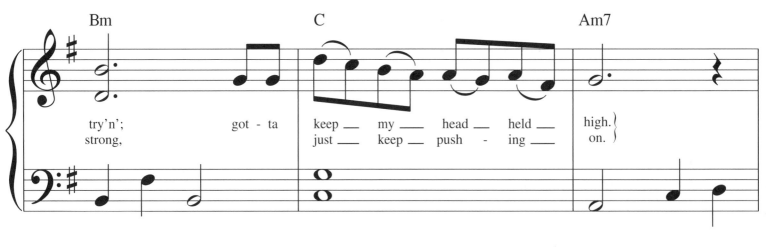

try'n'; got - ta keep __ my __ head __ held __ high.
strong, just __ keep __ push - ing __ on.

There's al-ways gon-na be an-oth-er moun-tain; I'm al-ways gon-na wan-na make it move.

Al-ways gon-na be an up-hill bat-tle; some-times, I'm gon-na have to lose.

Ain't a-bout how fast I get there; ain't a-bout what's wait-ing on the oth-er

1. Em   D   C   G

side; _____ it's the climb. _____

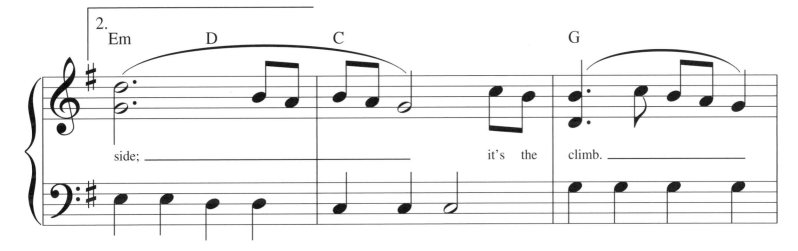

2. Em   D   C   G

side; _____ it's the climb. _____

Csus2

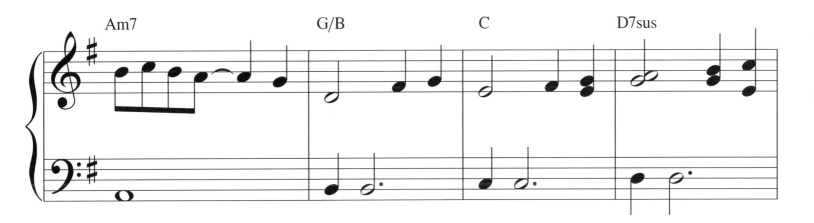

Am7   G/B   C   D7sus

There's al-ways gon-na be an-oth-er moun-tain; I'm al-ways gon-na wan-na make it move.

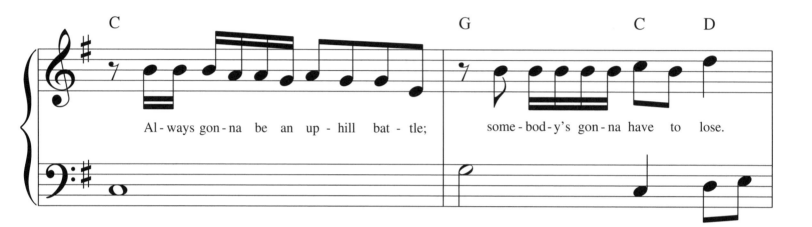

Al-ways gon-na be an up-hill bat-tle; some-bod-y's gon-na have to lose.

Ain't a-bout how fast I get there; ain't a-bout what's wait-ing on the oth-er

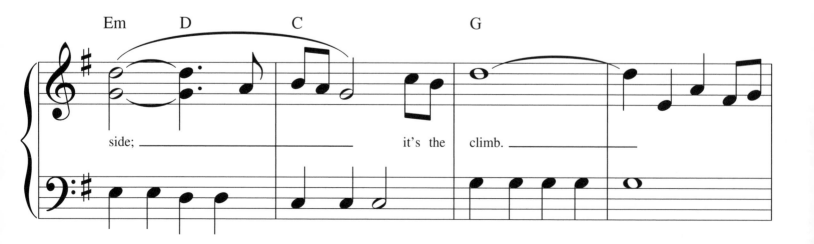

side; _____ it's the climb. _____

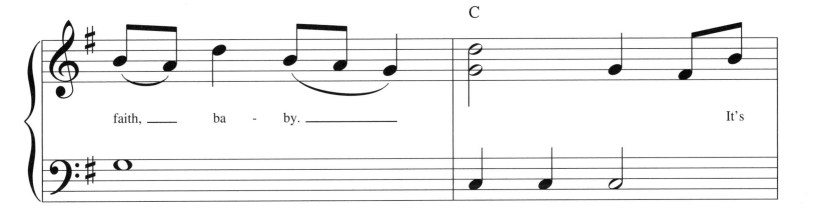

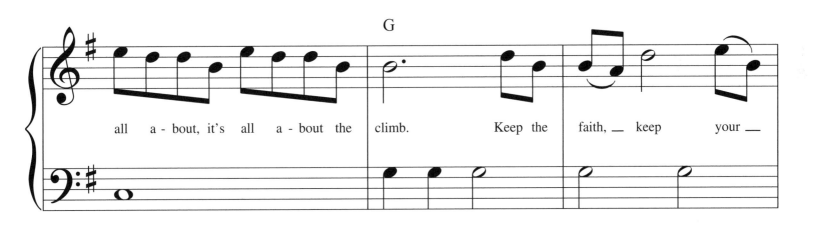

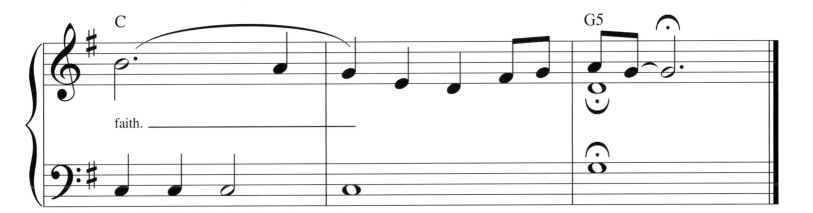

BRIDGE OVER TROUBLED WATER

Words and Music by
PAUL SIMON

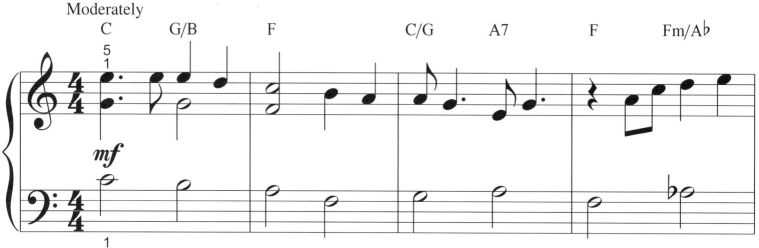

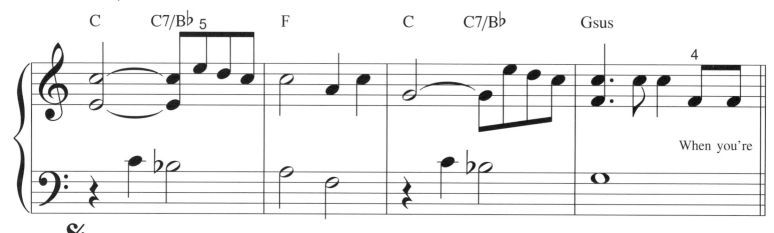

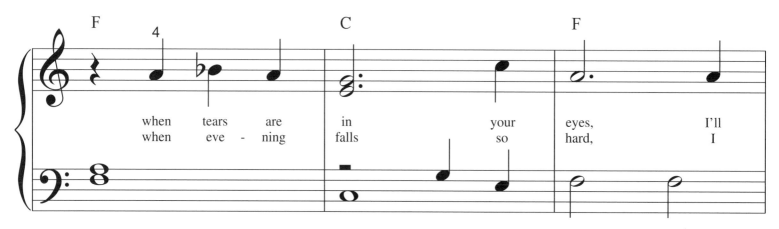

Copyright © 1969 Paul Simon (BMI)
Copyright Renewed
International Copyright Secured   All Rights Reserved
Used by Permission

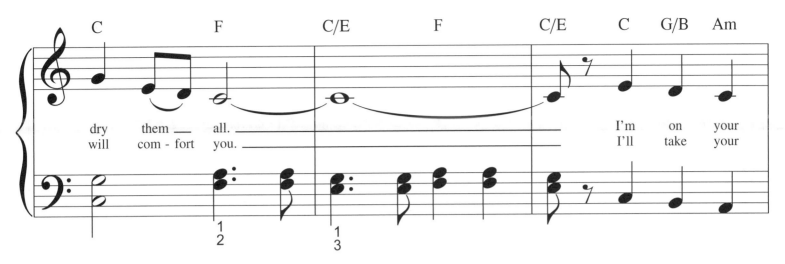

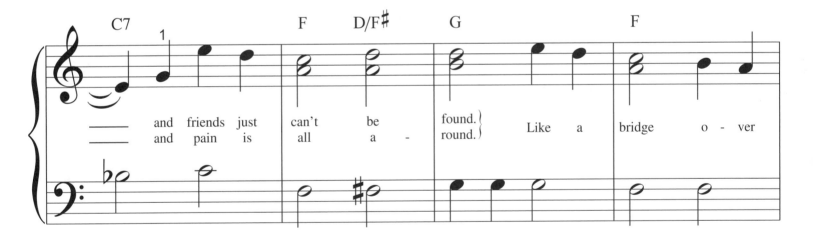

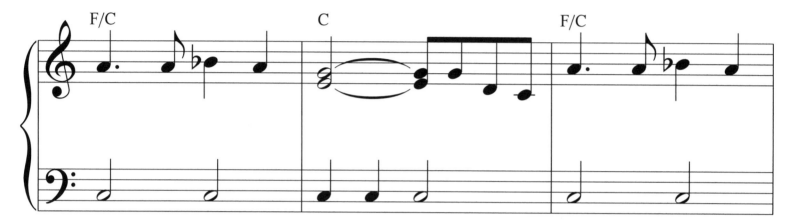

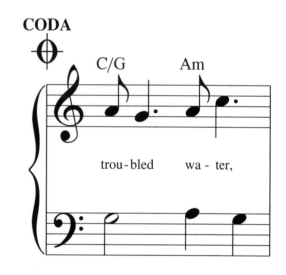

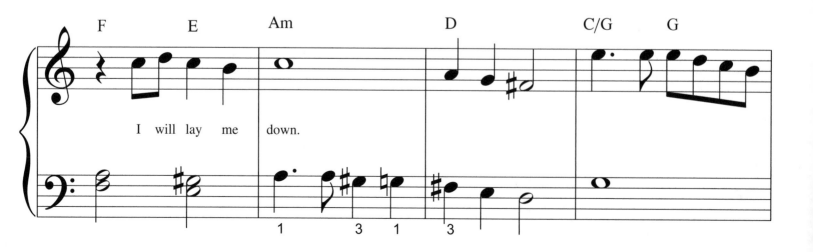

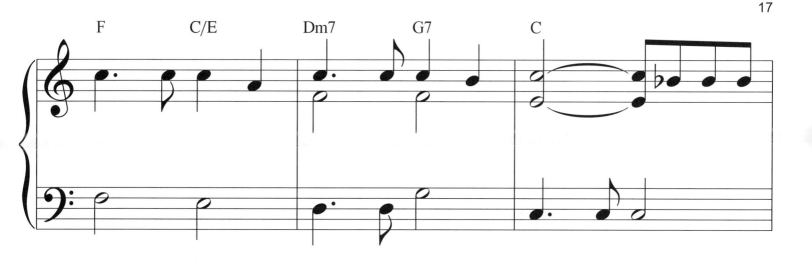

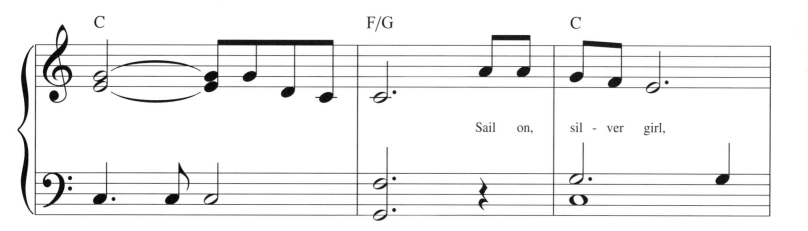

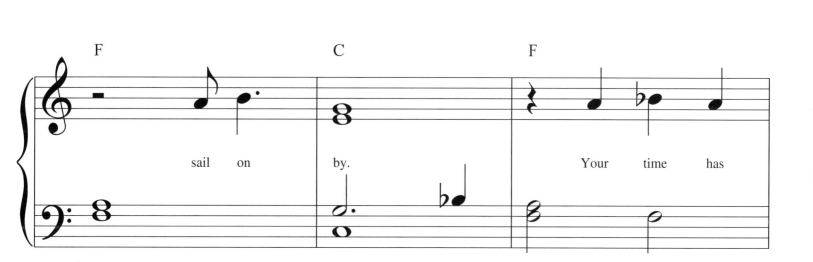

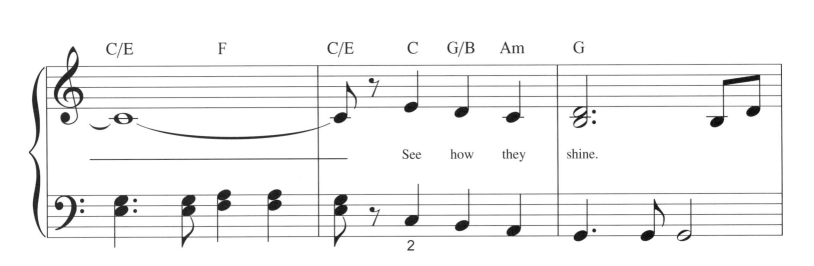

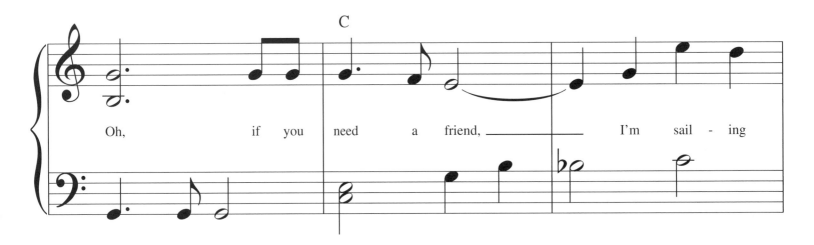

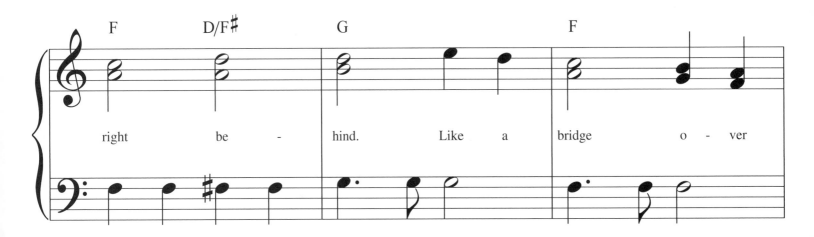

trou - bled wa - ter. I will ease your mind. Like a

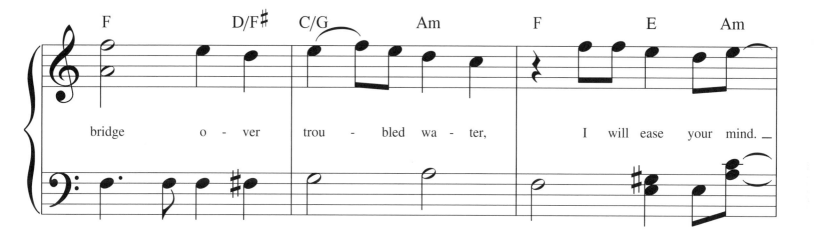

bridge o - ver trou - bled wa - ter, I will ease your mind.

rit.

FLY LIKE AN EAGLE

Words and Music by
STEVE MILLER

Moderately, in 2
N.C.

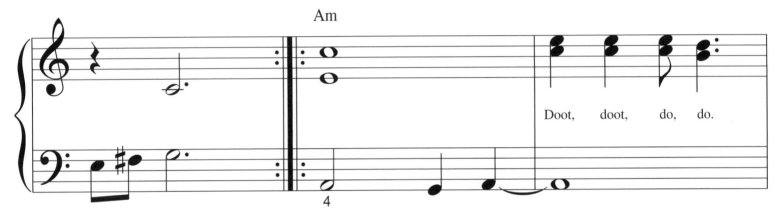

Doot,   doot,   do,   do.

Time   keeps   on

slip - pin',   slip - pin',   slip - pin' _____   in - to the fu -

Copyright © 1976 by Sailor Music
Copyright Renewed
All Rights Reserved   Used by Permission

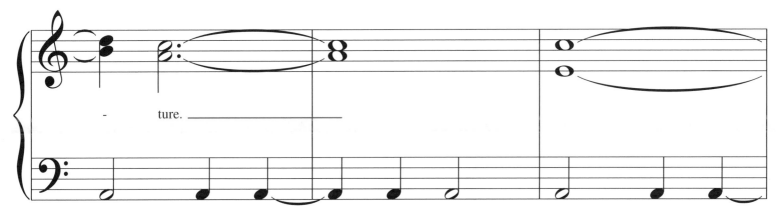

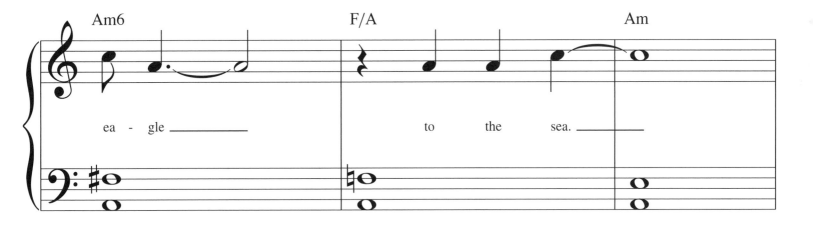

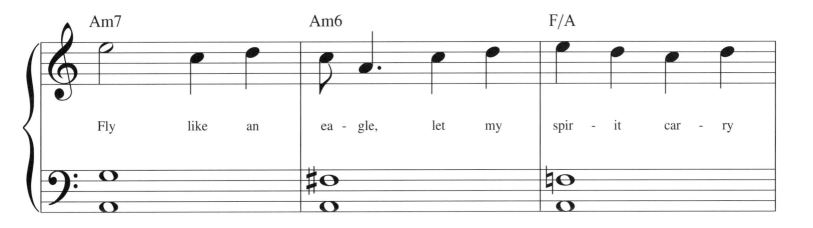

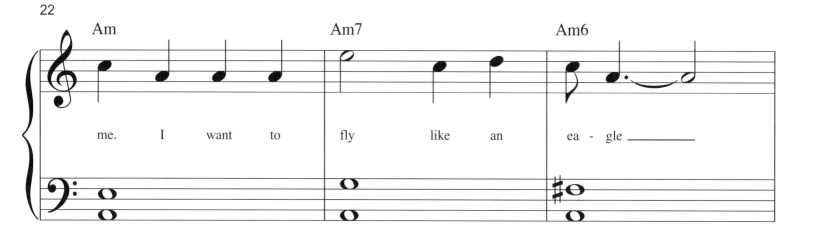

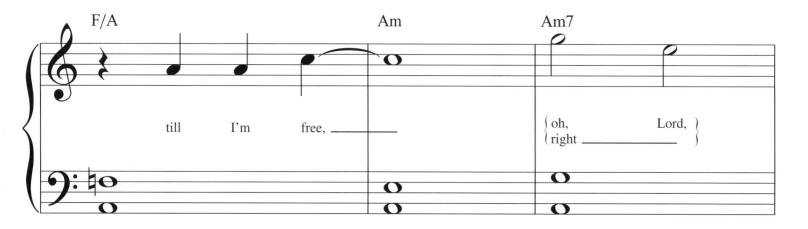

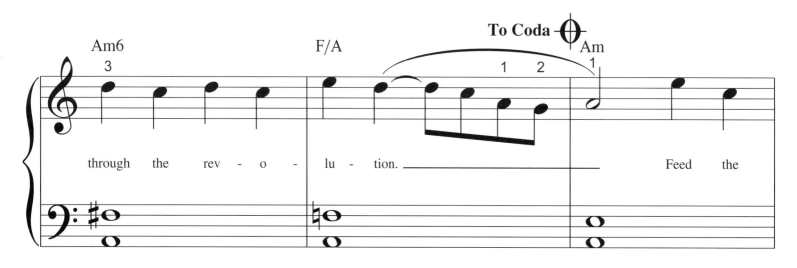

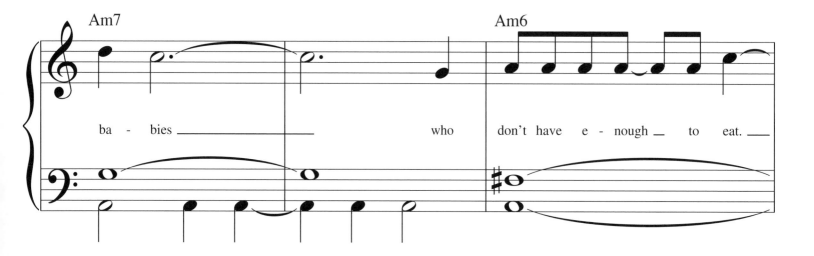

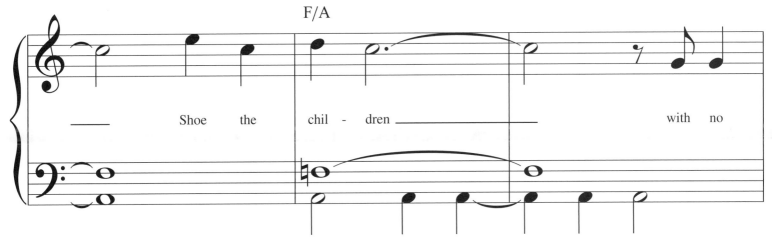

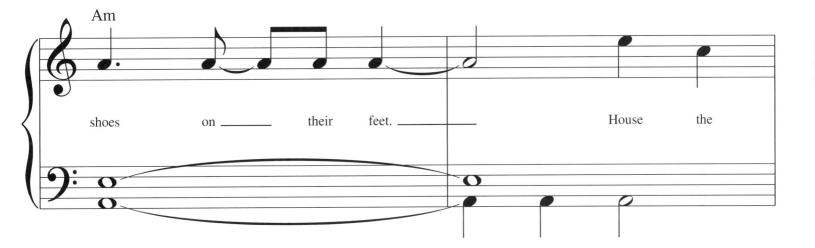

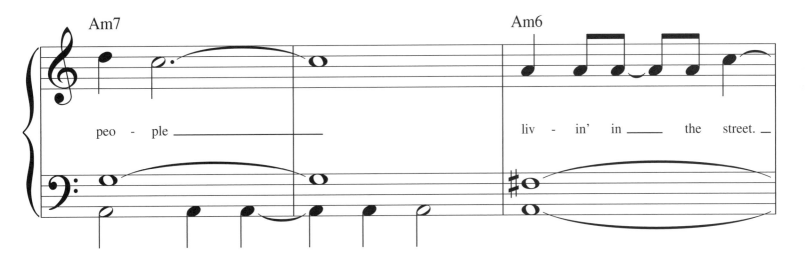

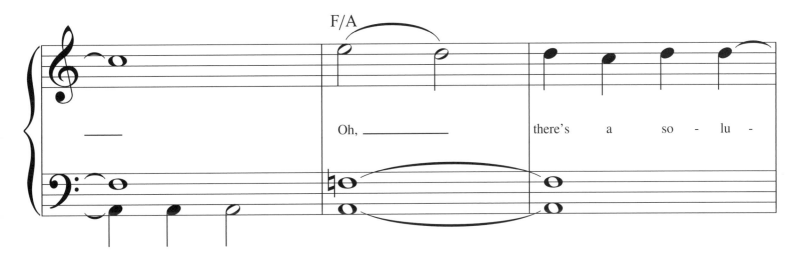

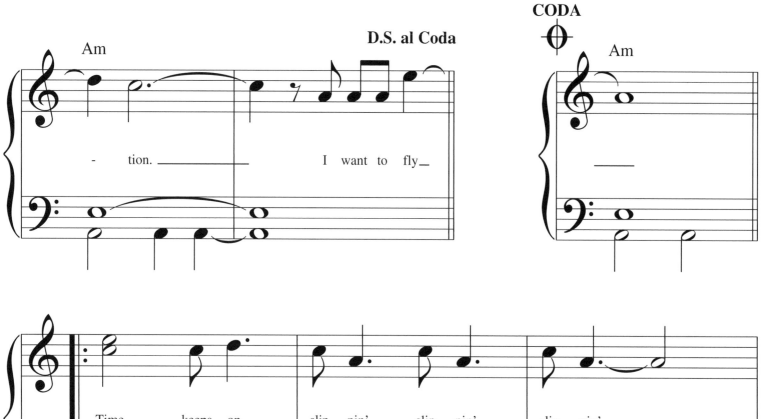

CODA

D.S. al Coda

Am

- tion. _____   I want to fly__

Am

_____

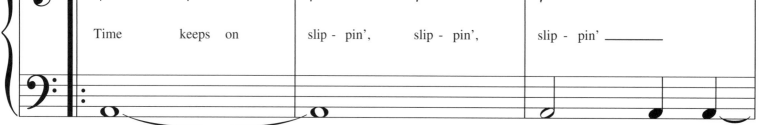

Time   keeps on   slip - pin',   slip - pin',   slip - pin' _____

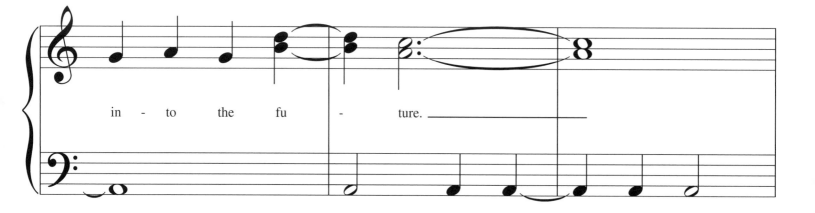

in - to   the   fu -   ture. _____

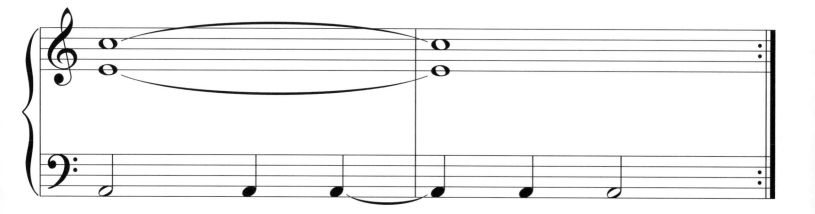

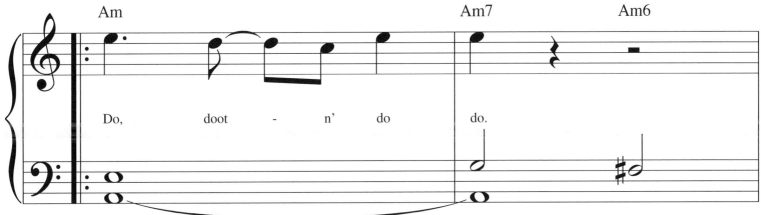

Do,   doot - n' do   do.

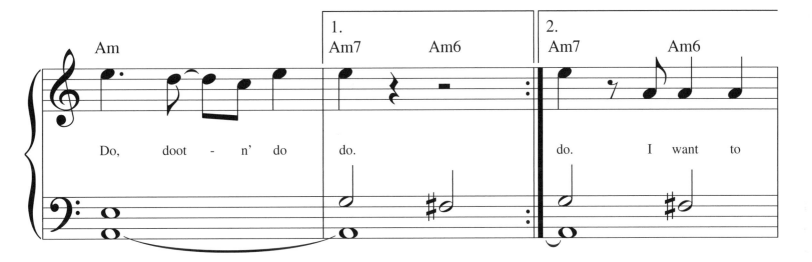

Do,   doot - n' do   do.   do.   I want to

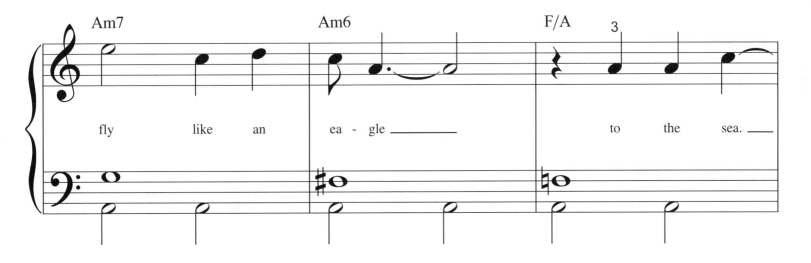

fly   like   an   ea - gle _____   to   the   sea. ___

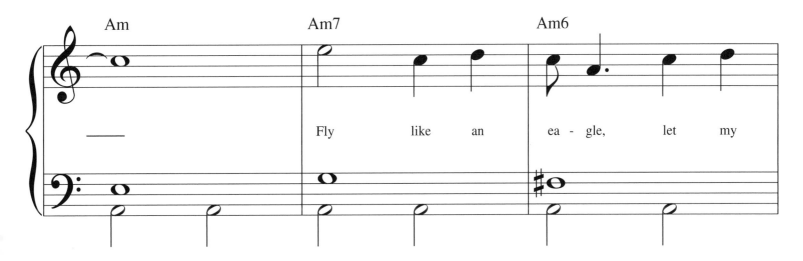

_____   Fly   like   an   ea - gle,   let   my

spir - it car - ry me. I want to fly like an

ea - gle _____ till I'm free, _____

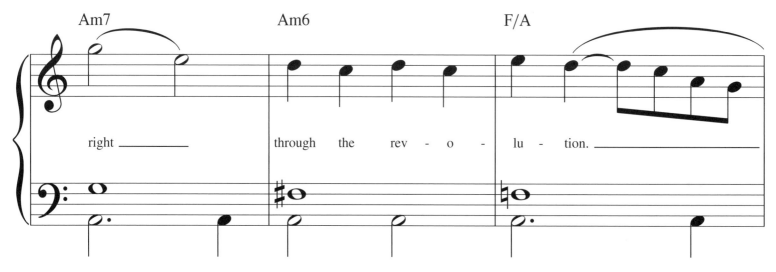

right _____ through the rev - o - lu - tion. _____

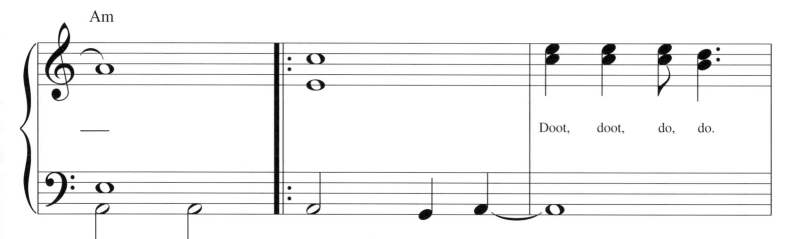

Doot, doot, do, do.

Time keeps on

1.

slip - pin', slip - pin', slip - pin' _____ in - to the fu -

- ture. _____

2.

G   Am

in - to the fu - ture.

FROM A DISTANCE

Words and Music by
JULIE GOLD

Copyright © 1986, 1987 Julie Gold Music (BMI) and Wing & Wheel Music (BMI)
Wing & Wheel Music Administered Worldwide by Irving Music, Inc.
International Copyright Secured   All Rights Reserved

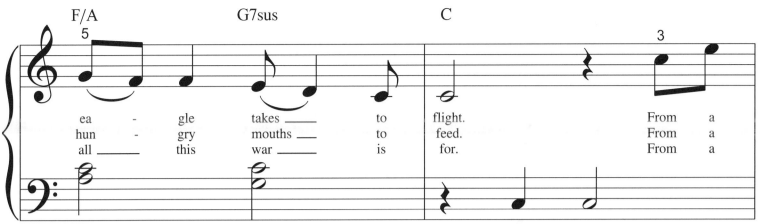

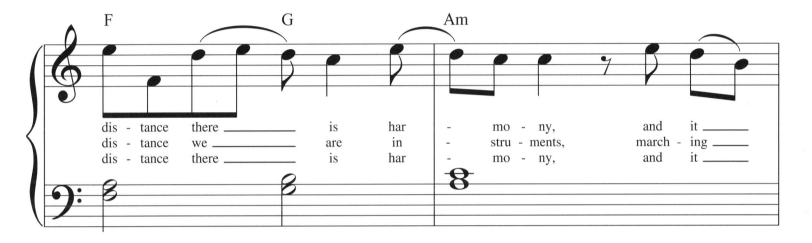

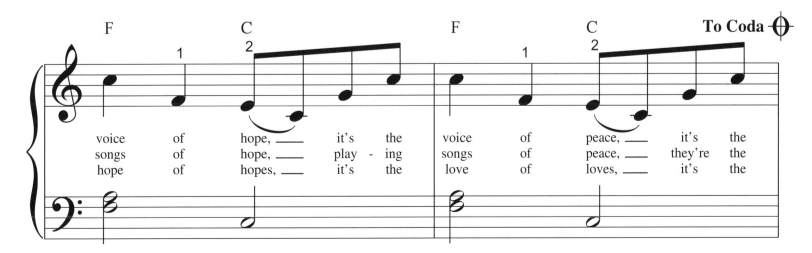

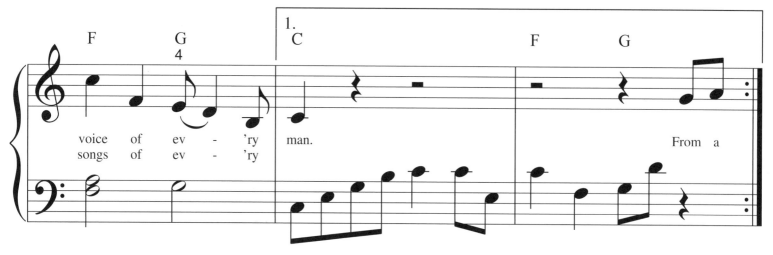

1.

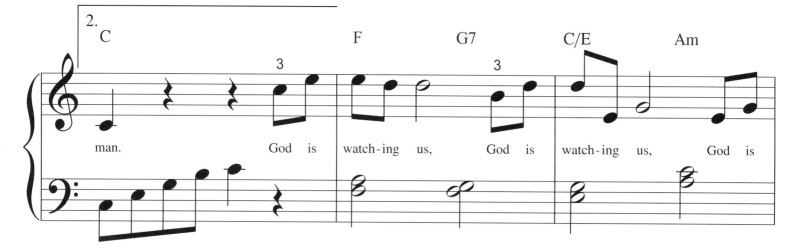

2.

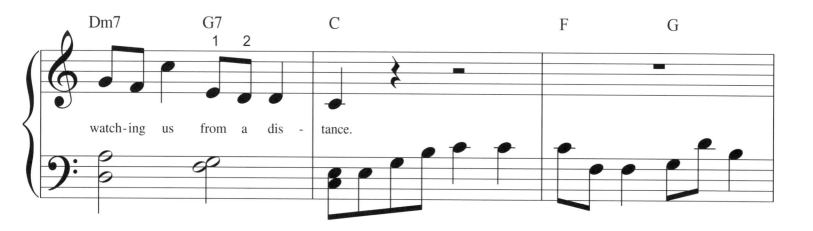

Instrumental solo

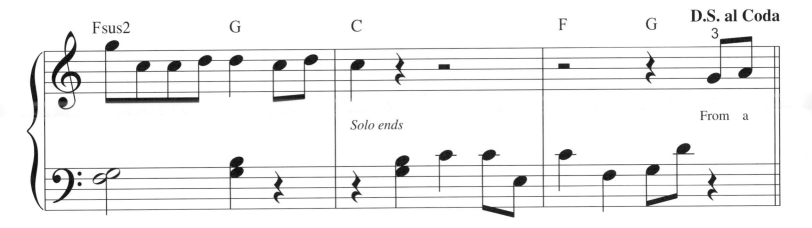

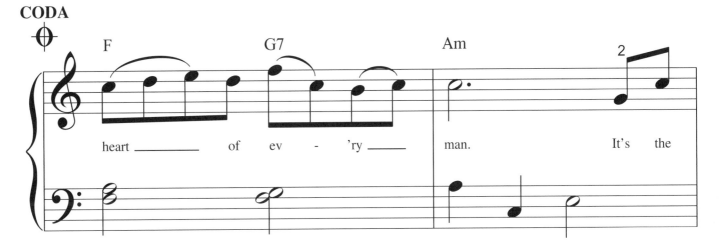

THE GREATEST LOVE OF ALL

Words by LINDA CREED
Music by MICHAEL MASSER

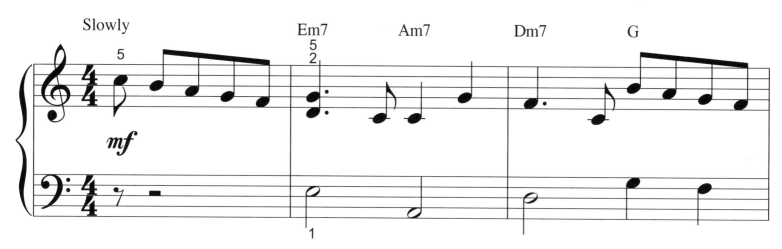

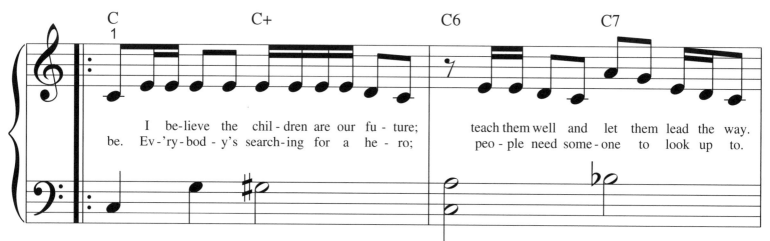

I be-lieve the chil-dren are our fu-ture;
teach them well and let them lead the way.

be. Ev-'ry-bod-y's search-ing for a he-ro;
peo-ple need some-one to look up to.

Show them all the beau-ty they pos-sess in - side.
Give them a

I nev-er found an-y-one who ful-filled my needs.
A lone-ly

© 1977 (Renewed) EMI GOLD HORIZON MUSIC CORP. and EMI GOLDEN TORCH MUSIC CORP.
All Rights Reserved   Used by Permission

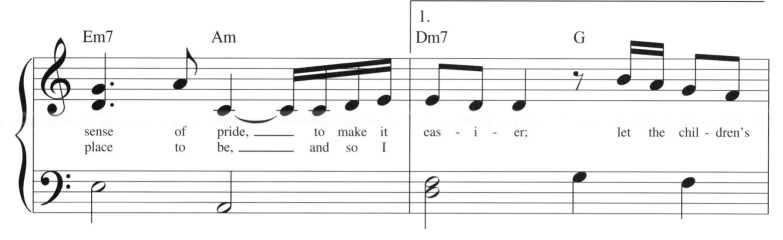

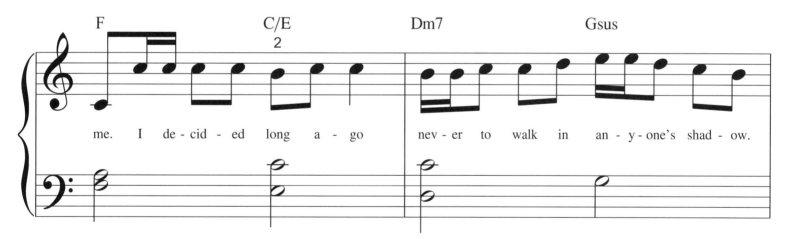

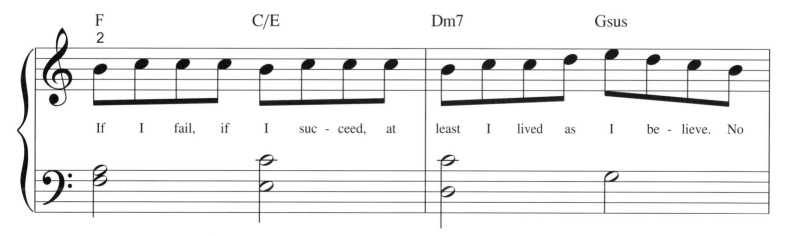

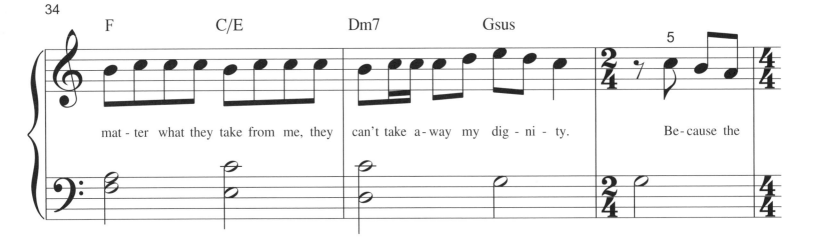

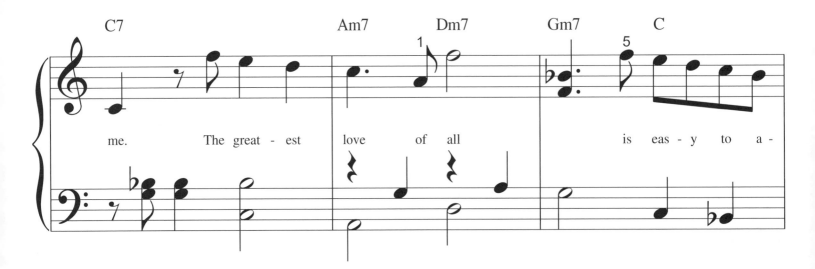

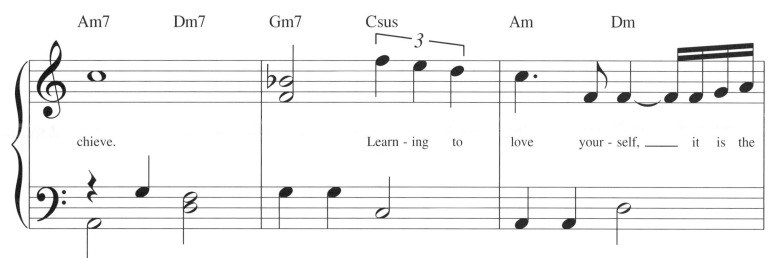

Am7 Dm7 Gm7 Csus Am Dm

chieve. Learn - ing to love your - self, _____ it is the

Gm7 B♭/C F G Em7 Am

great - est love of all. And if by chance that spe - cial place

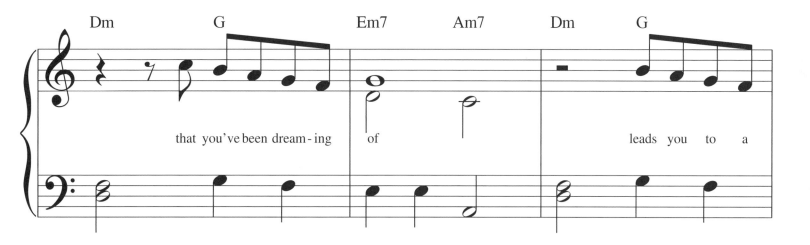

Dm G Em7 Am7 Dm G

that you've been dream - ing of leads you to a

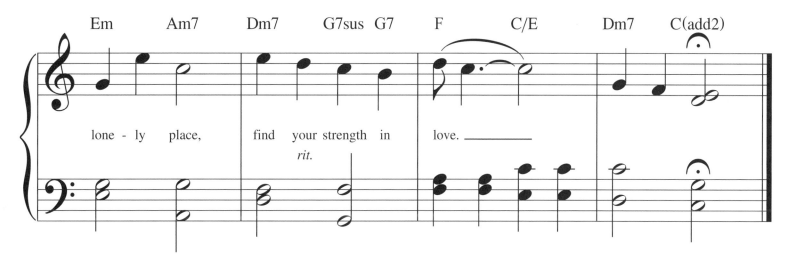

Em Am7 Dm7 G7sus G7 F C/E Dm7 C(add2)

lone - ly place, find your strength in love. _____

rit.

HE AIN'T HEAVY, HE'S MY BROTHER

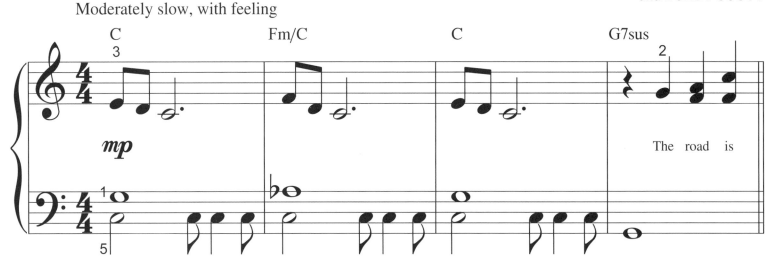

Words and Music by BOB RUSSELL
and BOBBY SCOTT

Moderately slow, with feeling

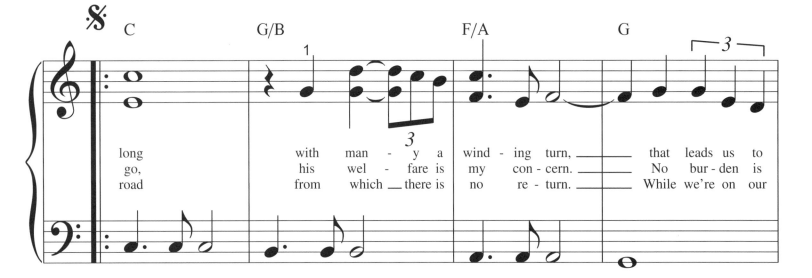

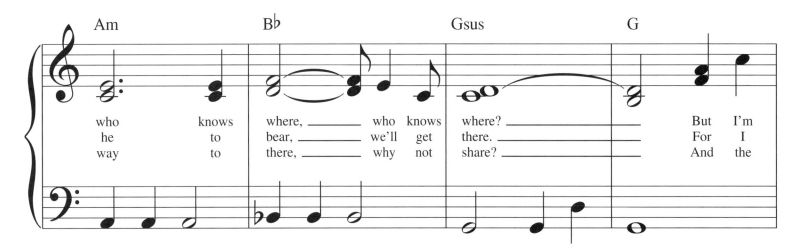

Copyright © 1969 Music Sales Corporation and Jenny Music
Copyright Renewed
International Copyright Secured   All Rights Reserved

37

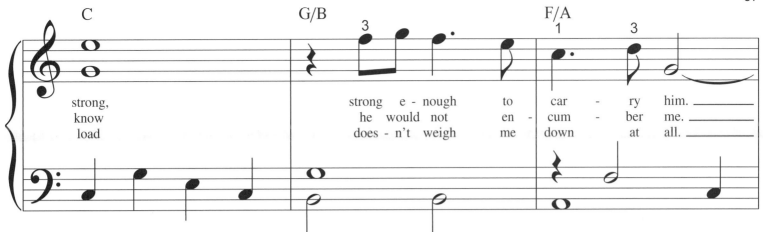

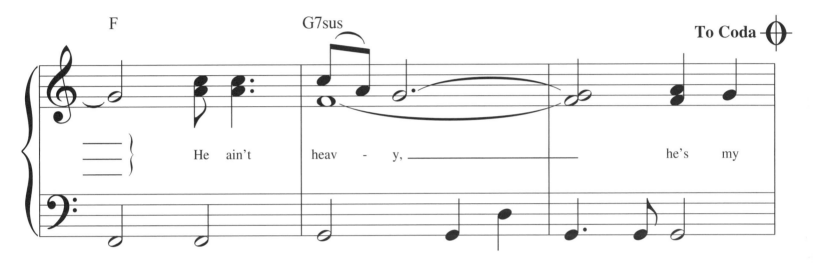

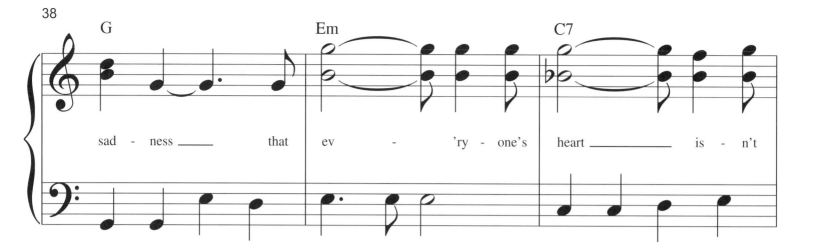

G   Em   C7

sad - ness _____ that ev - 'ry - one's heart _____ is - n't

Fmaj7   Esus   E   Am   F#m7♭5

filled _____ with the glad - ness _____ of love _____

D.S. al Coda

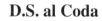

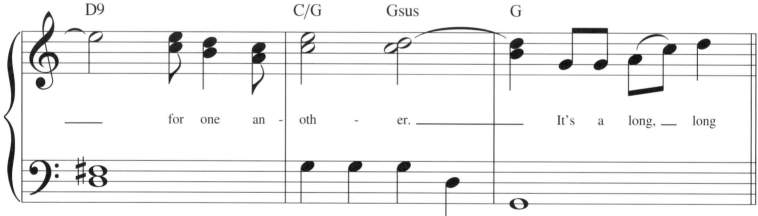

D9   C/G   Gsus   G

_____ for one an - oth - er. _____ It's a long, _ long

CODA

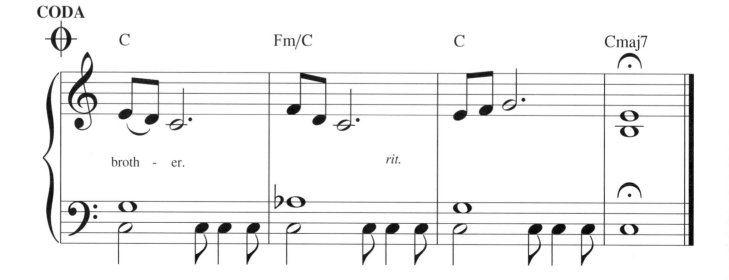

C   Fm/C   C   Cmaj7

broth - er.   *rit.*

HALLELUJAH

Words and Music by
LEONARD COHEN

Moderately, in 2

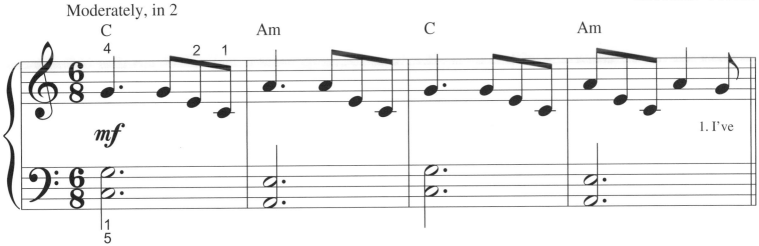

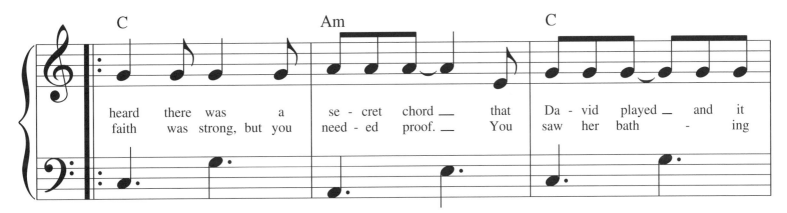

heard there was a se - cret chord ___ that Da - vid played ___ and it
faith was strong, but you need - ed proof. ___ You saw her bath ___ - ing

pleased the Lord, ___ but you don't ___ real - ly care for mu - sic, ___
on the roof. ___ Her beau - ty ___ and the moon - light o - ver -

do ya? ___ It goes like this: the fourth, the fifth, the
threw ya. ___ She tied you to her kitch - en chair, she

Copyright © 1995 Sony/ATV Music Publishing LLC
All Rights Administered by Sony/ATV Music Publishing LLC, 8 Music Square West, Nashville, TN 37203
International Copyright Secured   All Rights Reserved

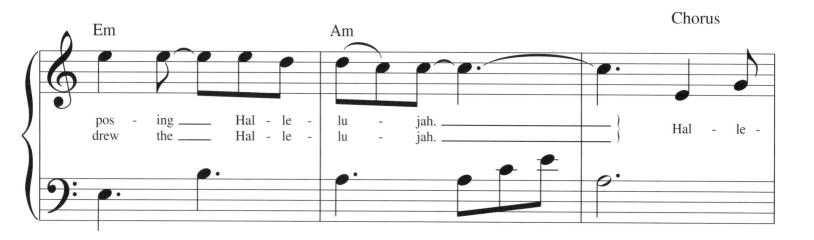

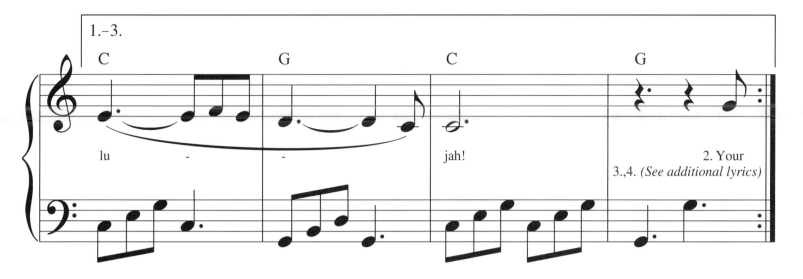

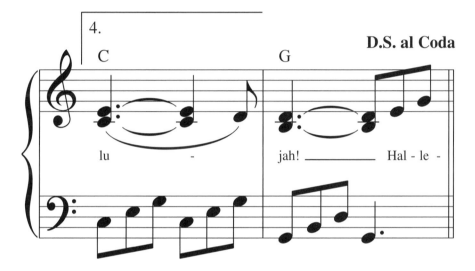

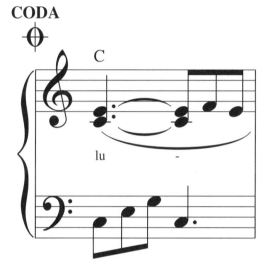

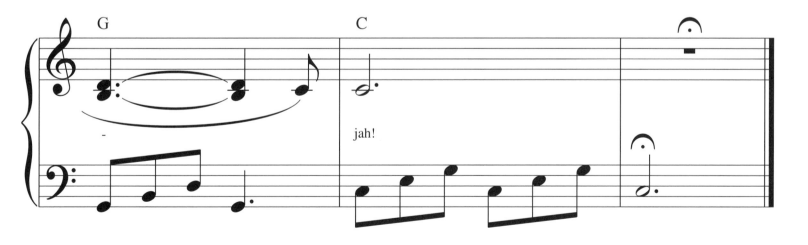

Additional Lyrics

3. You say I took the Name in vain.
I don't even know the Name,
But if I did, well, really, what's it to ya?
There's a blaze of light in every word.
It doesn't matter which are heard,
The holy or the broken Hallelujah.
Chorus

4. I did my best; it wasn't much.
I couldn't feel, so I tried to touch.
I've told the truth; I didn't come to fool ya.
And even though it all went wrong,
I'll stand before the Lord of Song
With nothing on my tongue but Hallelujah.
Chorus

HEAL THE WORLD

Written and Composed by
MICHAEL JACKSON

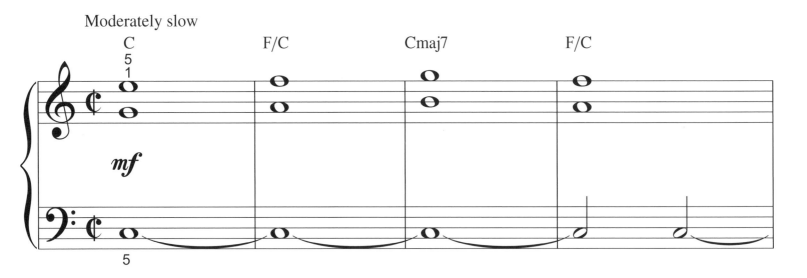

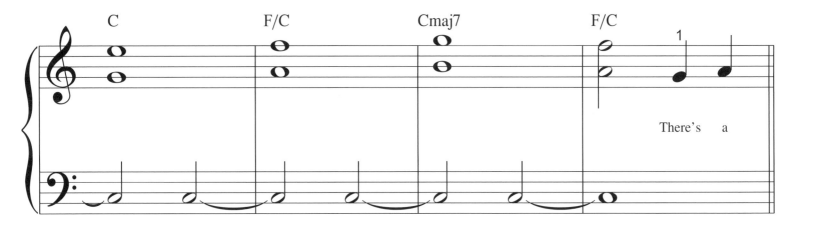

Copyright © 1991 Mijac Music
All Rights Administered by Sony/ATV Music Publishing LLC, 8 Music Square West, Nashville, TN 37203
International Copyright Secured   All Rights Reserved

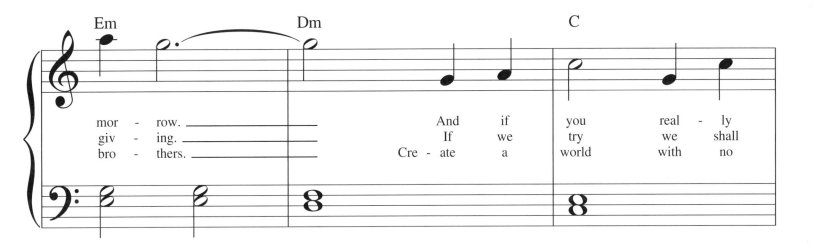

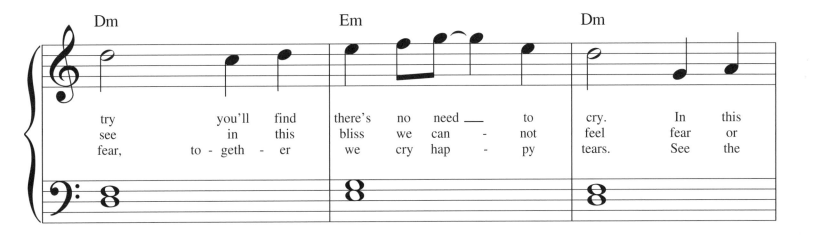

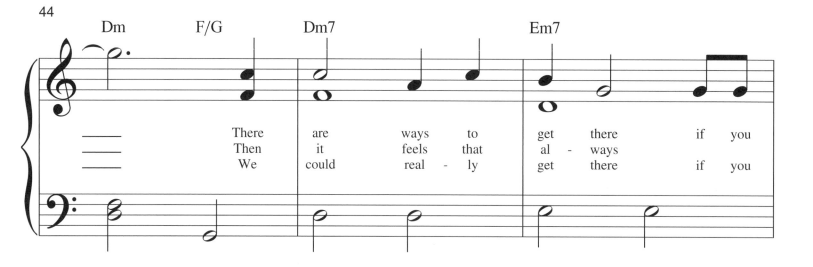

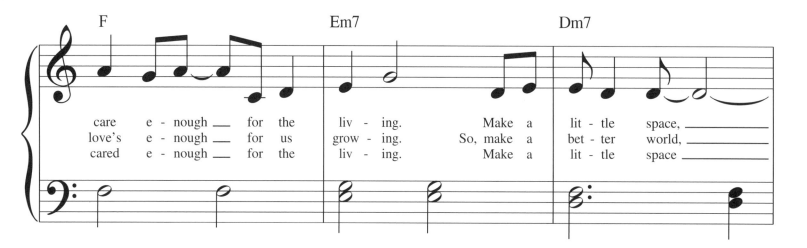

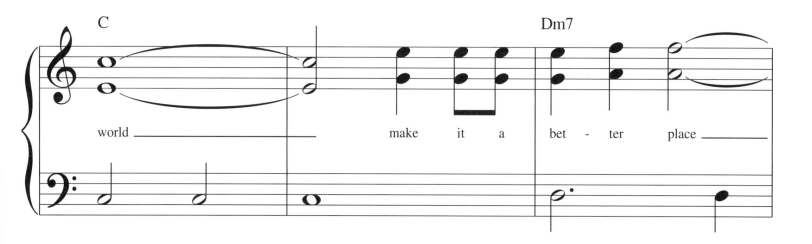

for you and ___ for me ___ and the

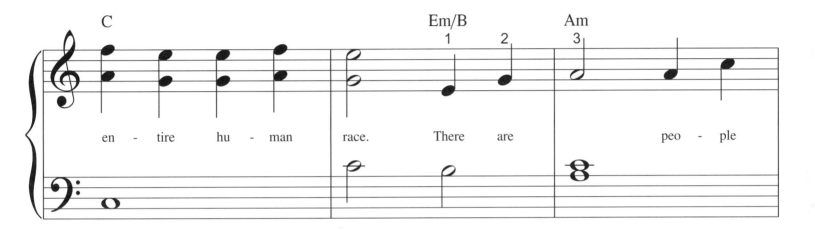

en - tire hu - man race. There are peo - ple

dy - ing; if you care e - nough ___ for the liv - ing, make a

bet - ter place ___ for you and ___ for me.

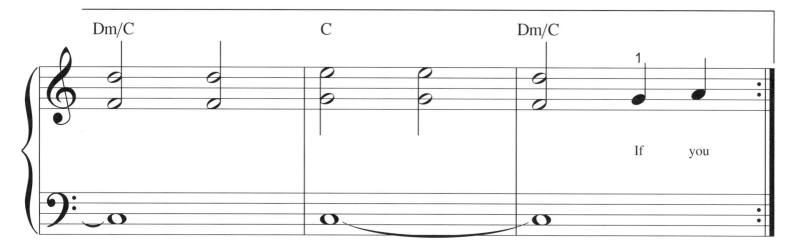

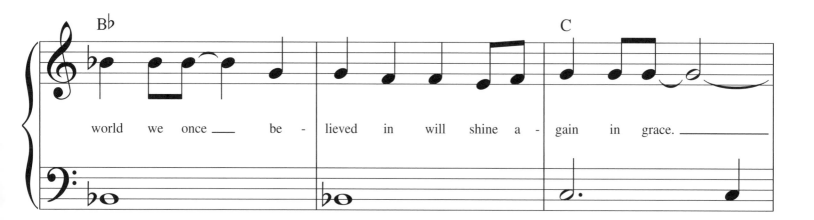

Then why do we ___ keep stran - gling life, wound this

earth, ___ cru - ci - fy its soul? Though it's plain to see ___ this world is

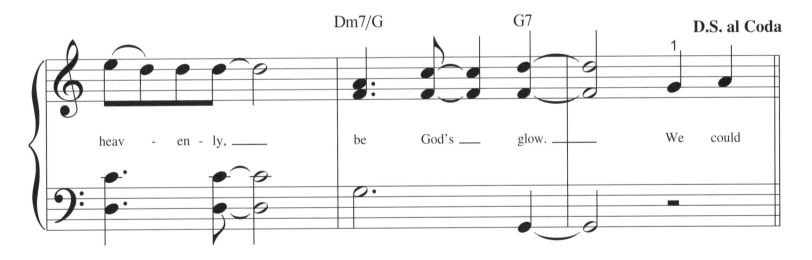

heav - en - ly, ___ be God's ___ glow. ___ We could

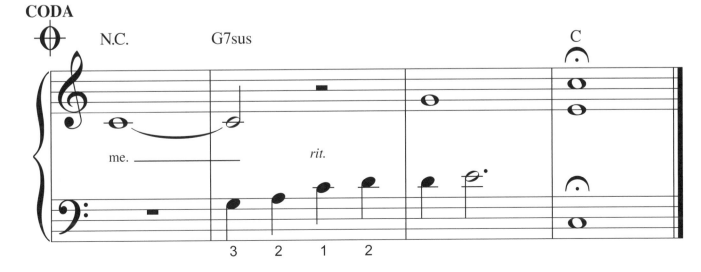

me. ___ rit. ___

I BELIEVE I CAN FLY

Words and Music by
ROBERT KELLY

Moderately, in 2

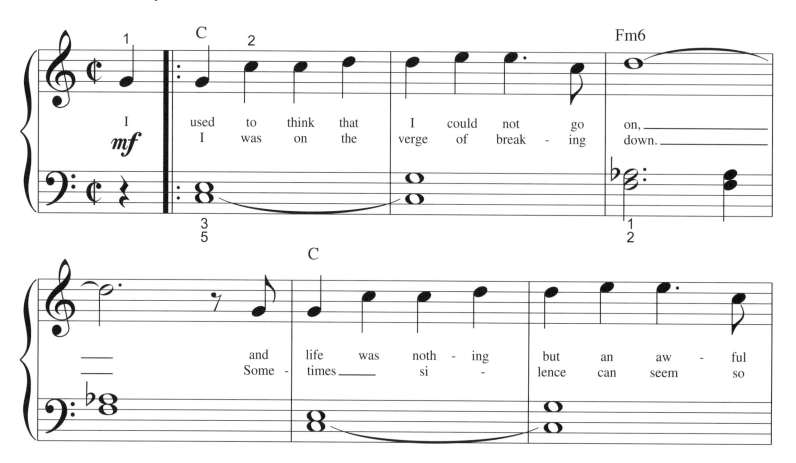

Copyright © 1996 by Universal Music - Z Songs and R. Kelly Publishing
All Rights Administered by Universal Music - Z Songs
International Copyright Secured   All Rights Reserved

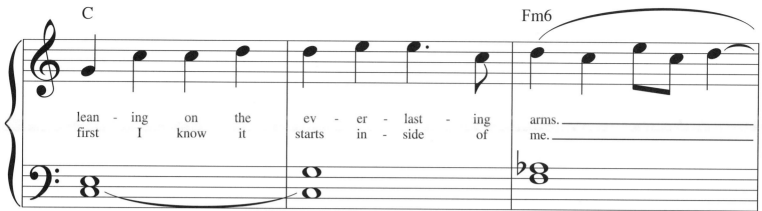

lean - ing on the ev - er - last - ing arms. _____
first I know it starts in - side of me. _____

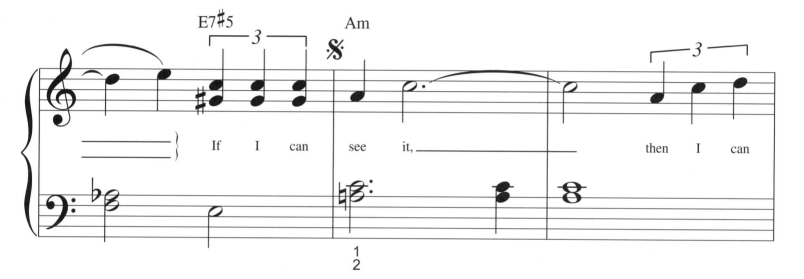

If I can see it, _____ then I can

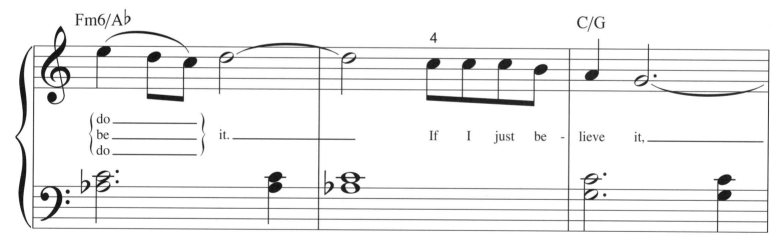

do _____
be _____ it. _____ If I just be - lieve it, _____
do _____

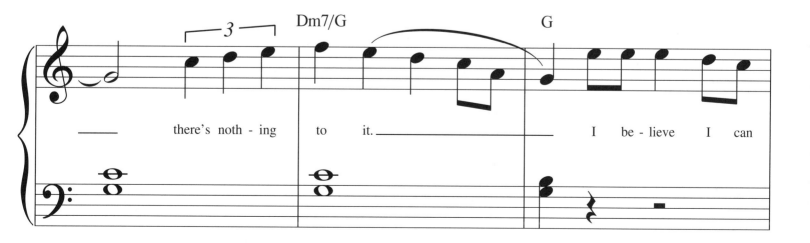

_____ there's noth - ing to it. _____ I be - lieve I can

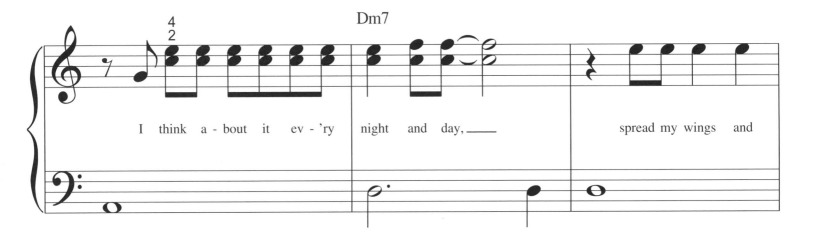

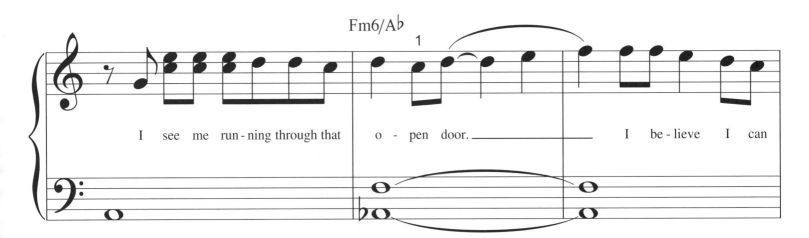

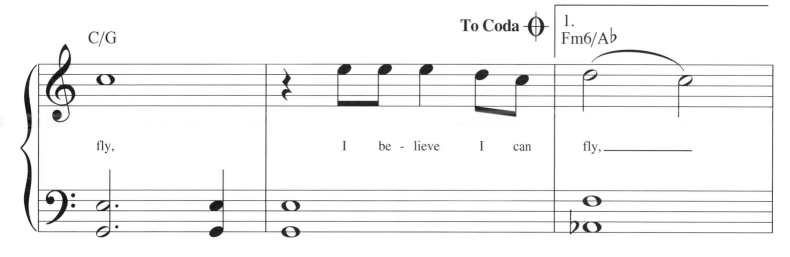

fly,   I be - lieve I can   fly, _____

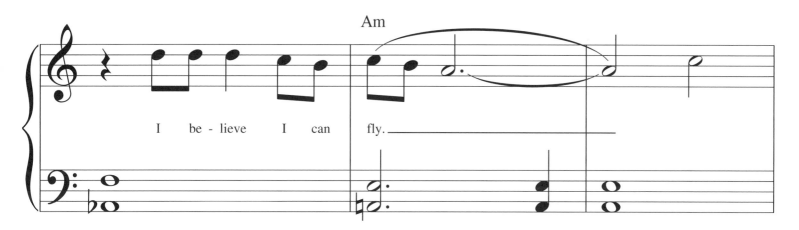

I be - lieve I can fly. _____

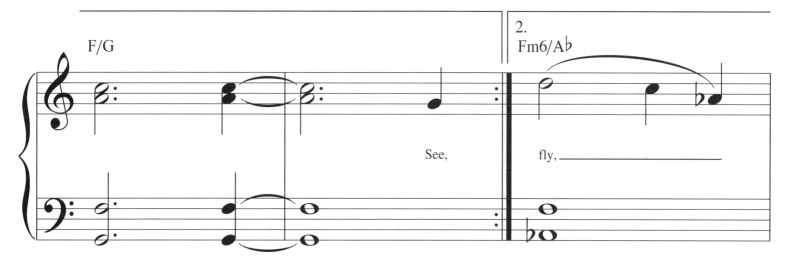

See,   fly, _____

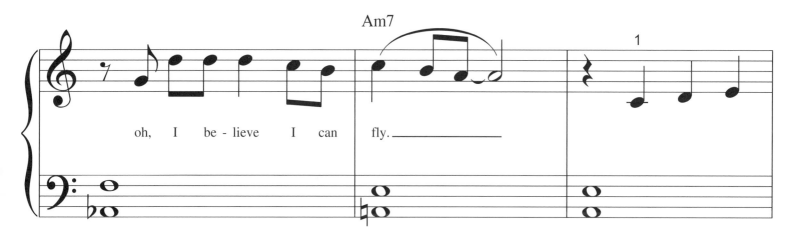

oh, I be - lieve I can fly. _____

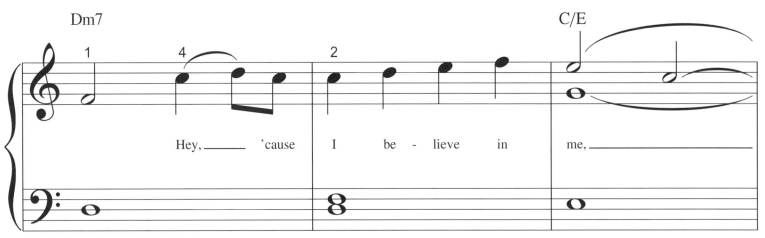

Dm7
C/E

Hey, ____ 'cause I be - lieve in me, _____

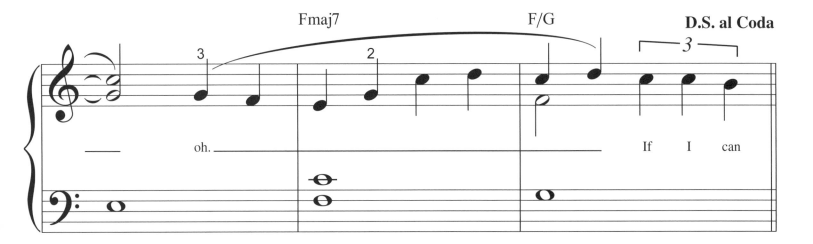

Fmaj7
F/G
D.S. al Coda

___ oh. _____ If I can

CODA
Fm6/A♭
C/G

fly, _____ I be - lieve I can fly. _____

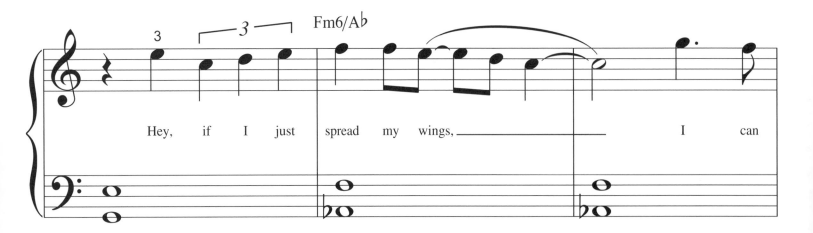

Fm6/A♭

Hey, if I just spread my wings, _____ I can

53

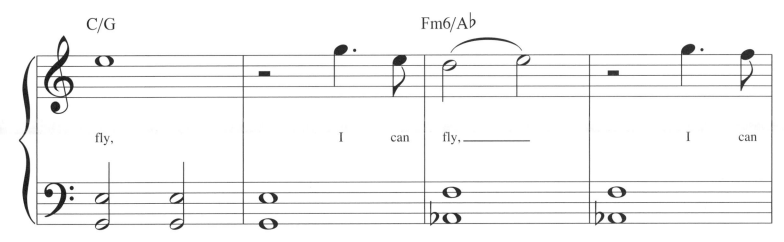

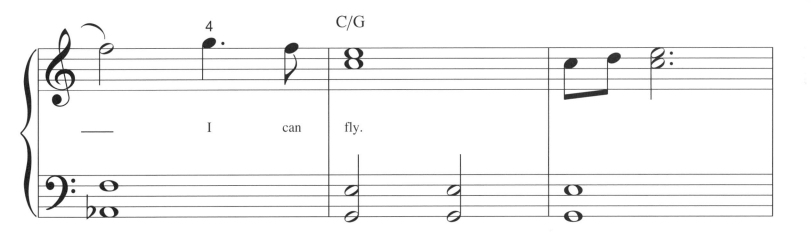

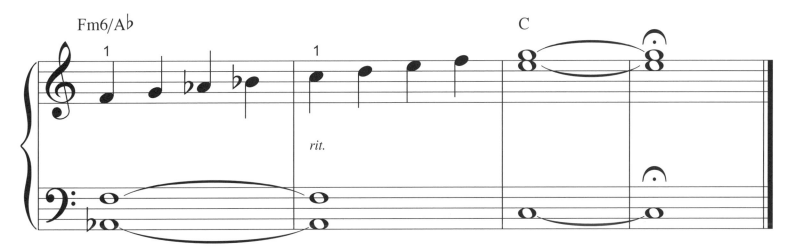

I'D LIKE TO TEACH
THE WORLD TO SING

Words and Music by BILL BACKER,
ROQUEL DAVIS, ROGER COOK
and ROGER GREENAWAY

I'd like to build ___ the world a home ___ and fur - nish it with love, ___

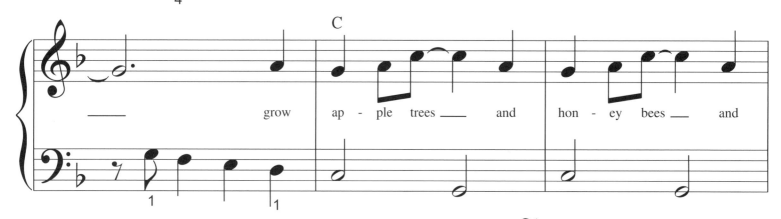

___ grow ap - ple trees ___ and hon - ey bees ___ and

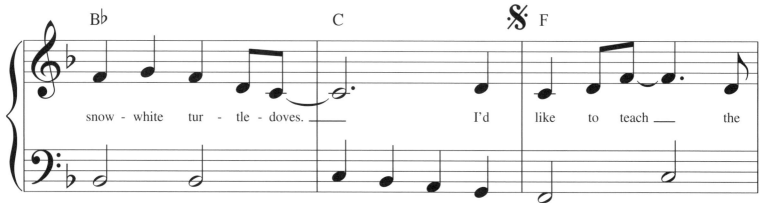

snow - white tur - tle - doves. ___ I'd like to teach ___ the

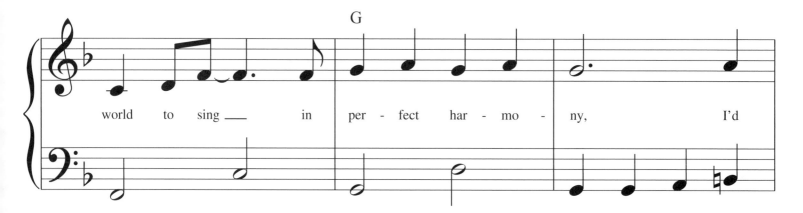

world to sing ___ in per - fect har - mo - ny, I'd

© 1971, 1972 (Copyrights Renewed) SHADA MUSIC, INC.
All Rights Reserved   Used by Permission

C ... B♭

like to hold it in my arms ____ and keep it com - pa - ny. ____

F ... 3 ... 3

____ I'd like to see the world ____ for once all

G ... 3 ... C

stand - ing hand in hand, and hear them ech - o

To Coda

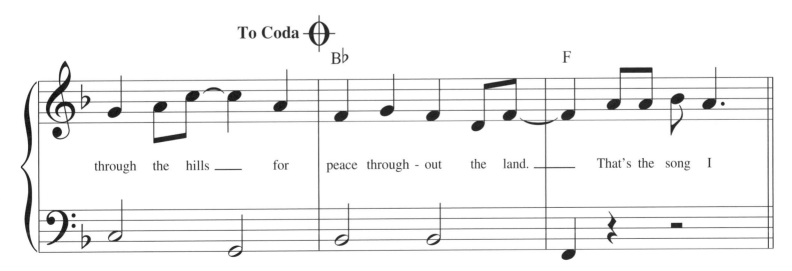

B♭ ... F

through the hills ____ for peace through - out the land. ____ That's the song I

F

G

hear, let the world sing to - day;

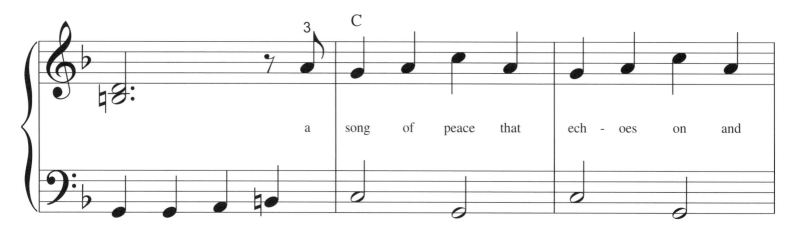

C

a song of peace that ech - oes on and

1. Bb

F

2. Bb

nev - er goes a - way. That's the song I

nev - er goes a - way.

C **D.S. al Coda**

I'd

CODA

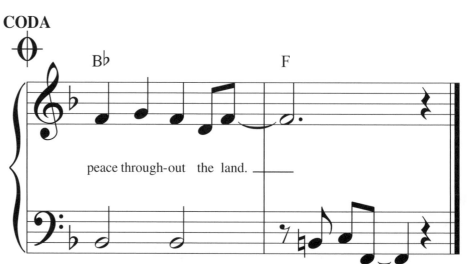

Bb

F

peace through-out the land.

LEAN ON ME

Words and Music by
BILL WITHERS

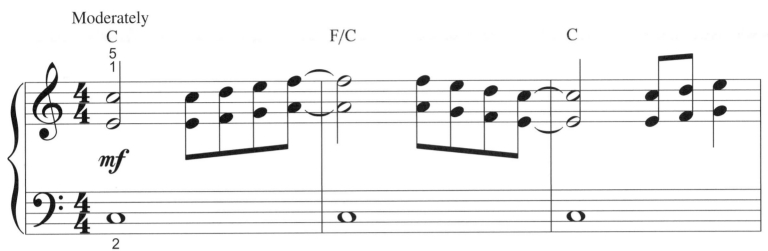

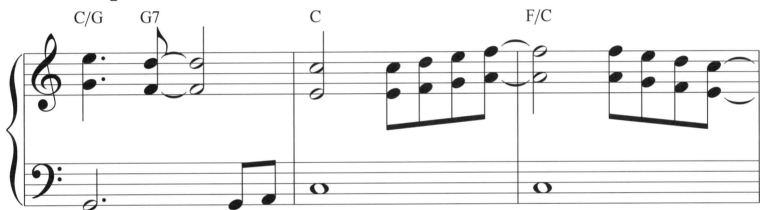

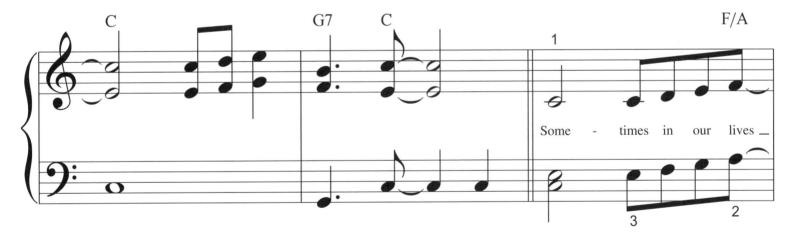

Some - times in our lives _

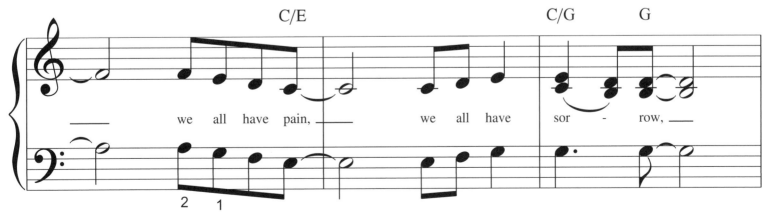

_ we all have pain, _ we all have sor - row, _

Copyright © 1972 INTERIOR MUSIC CORP.
Copyright Renewed
All Rights Controlled and Administered by SONGS OF UNIVERSAL, INC.
All Rights Reserved   Used by Permission

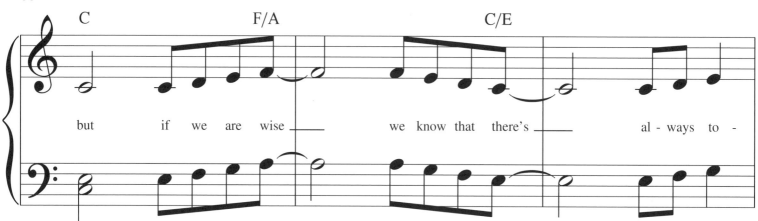

but if we are wise ____ we know that there's ____ al - ways to -

mor - row. ____ Lean on me ____ when you're not strong, ____ and I'll be your friend; _

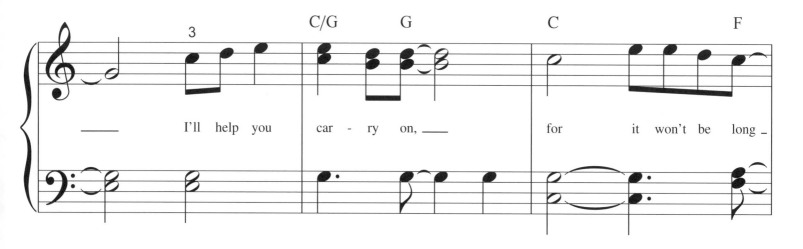

____ I'll help you car - ry on, ____ for it won't be long _

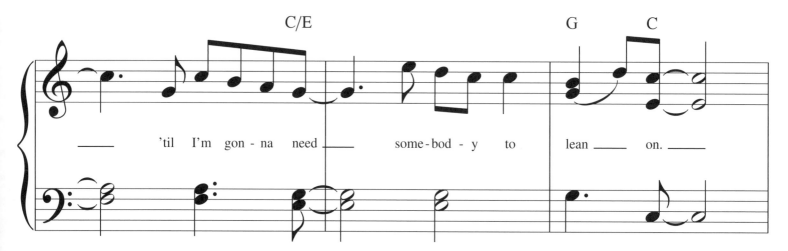

____ 'til I'm gon - na need ____ some - bod - y to lean ____ on. ____

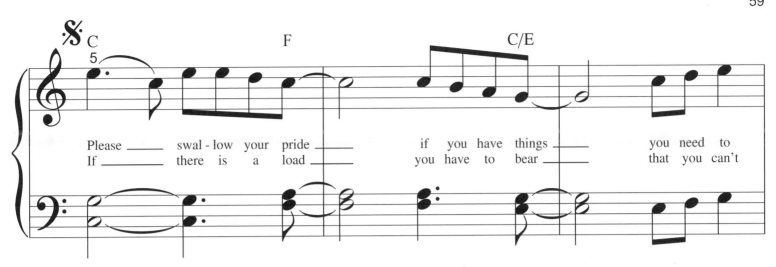

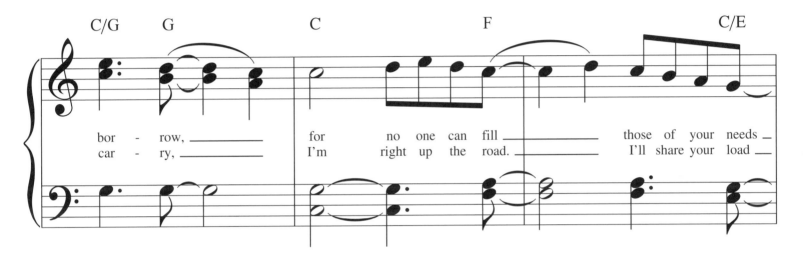

lean ___ on. ___ I just might have a prob-lem that you'll un - der - stand. ___ We all

need some-bod - y to lean ___ on. ___ Lean on me ___ when you're not strong, ___

___ and I'll be your friend; ___ I'll help you car - ry on, ___

for it won't be long ___ 'til I'm gon - na need ___ some-bod - y to

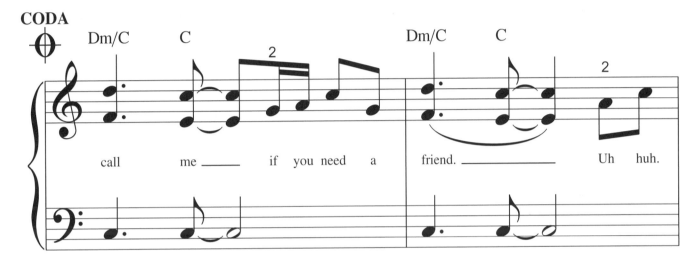

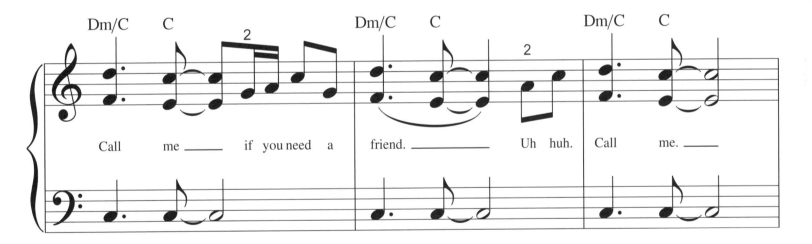

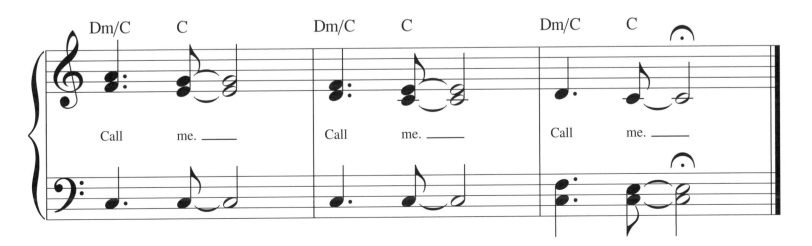

IMAGINE

Written by
JOHN LENNON

© 1971 (Renewed) LENONO MUSIC
All Rights Administered by DOWNTOWN DMP SONGS/DOWNTOWN MUSIC PUBLISHING LLC
All Rights Reserved   Used by Permission

a - bove us on - ly sky.

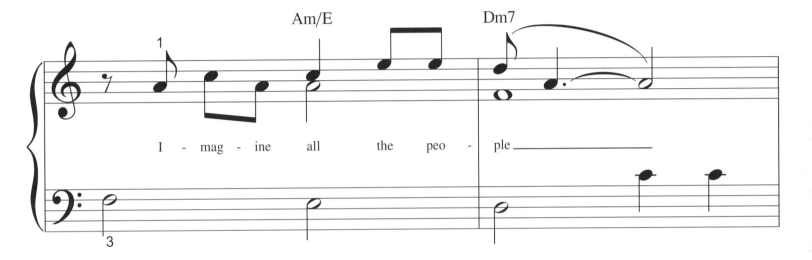

I - mag - ine all the peo - ple

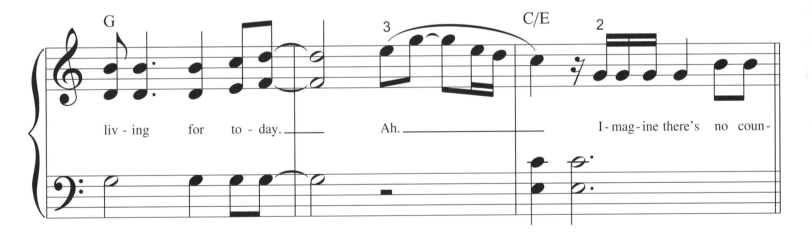

liv - ing for to - day. Ah. I - mag - ine there's no coun-

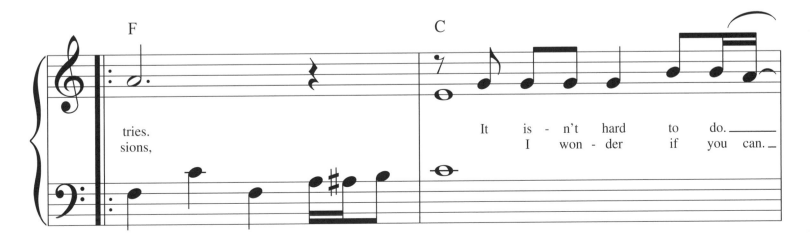

tries.
sions,

It is - n't hard to do.
I won - der if you can.

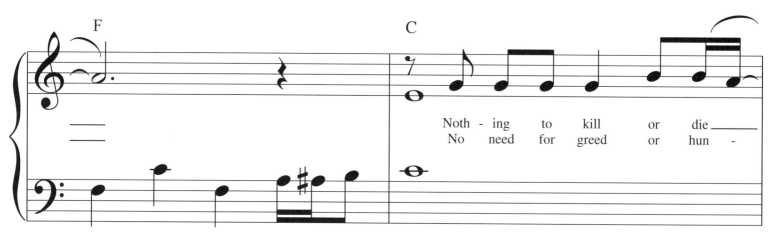

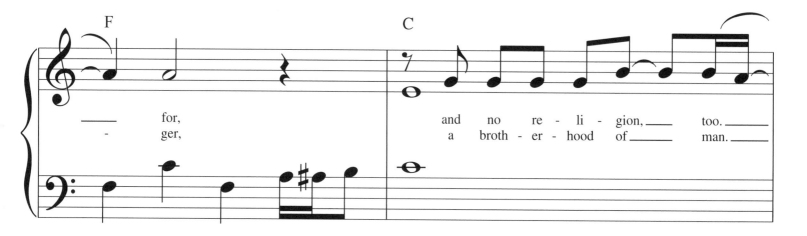

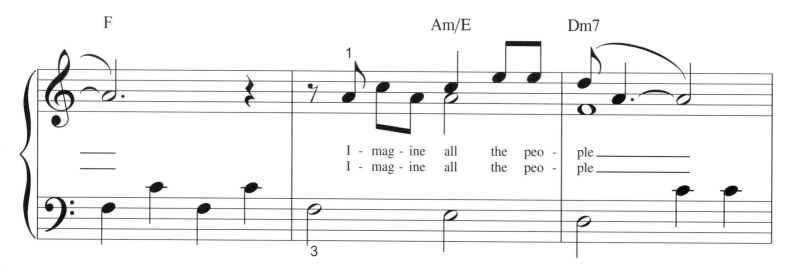

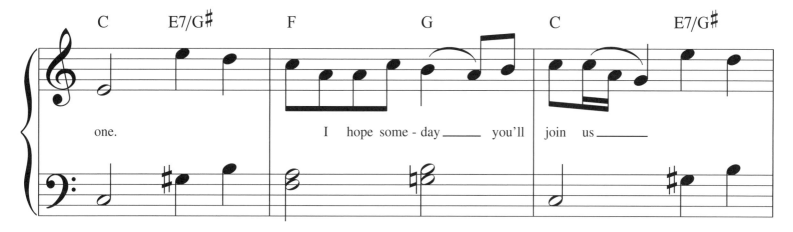

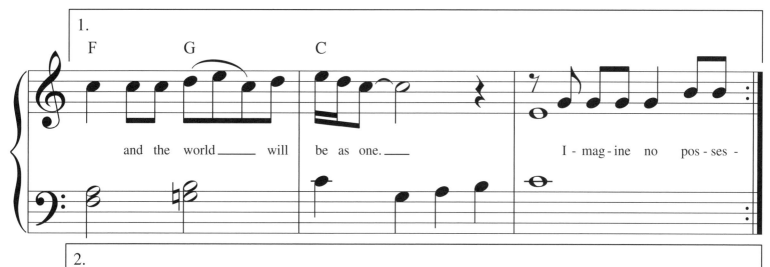

LET THERE BE PEACE ON EARTH

Words and Music by SY MILLER
and JILL JACKSON

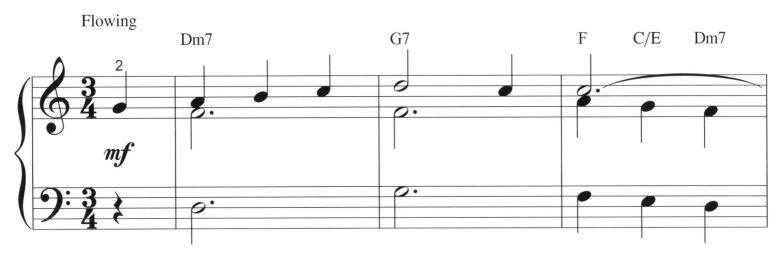

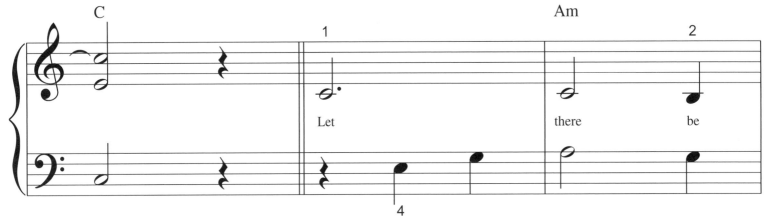

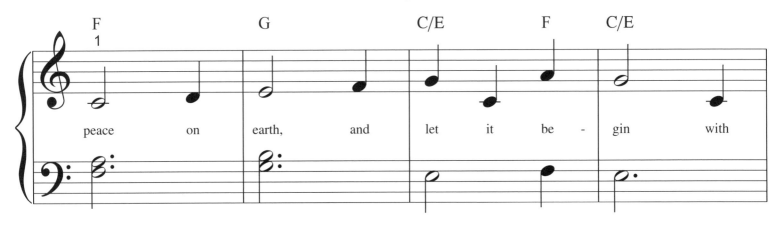

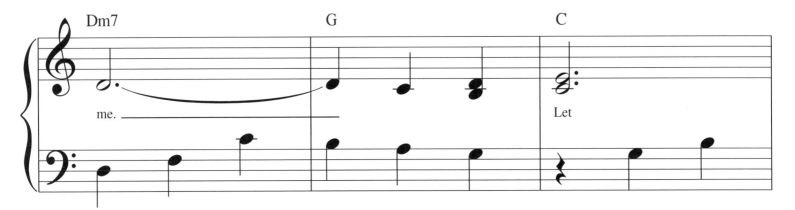

Copyright © 1955 by Jan-Lee Music (ASCAP)
Copyright Renewed 1983
International Copyright Secured   All Rights Reserved
Used by Permission

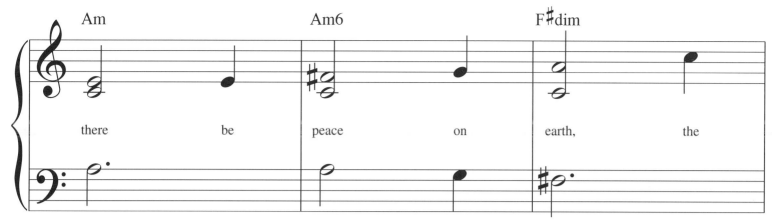

there be peace on earth, the

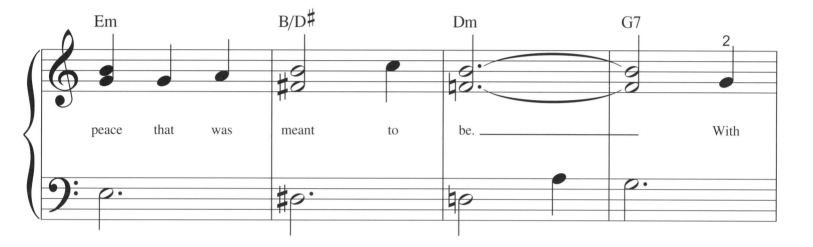

peace that was meant to be. _____ With

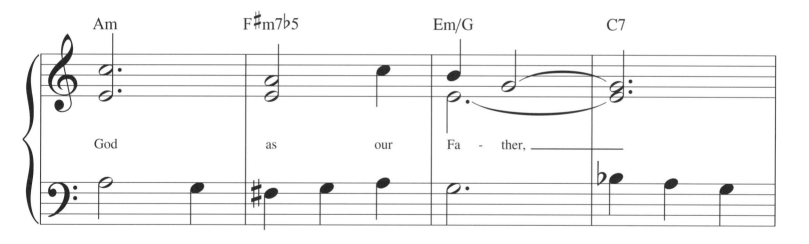

God as our Fa - ther, _____

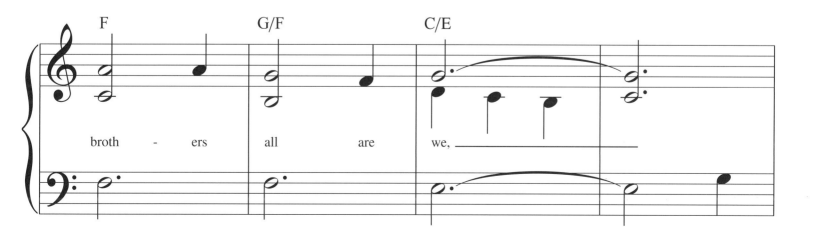

broth - ers all are we, _____

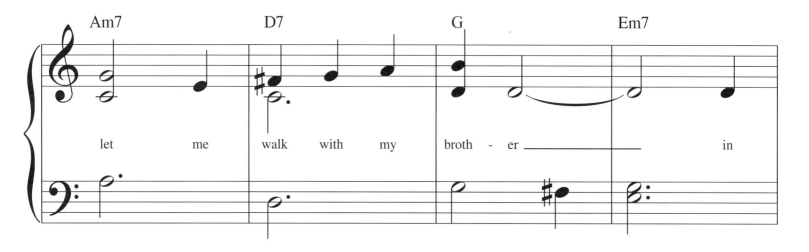

let me walk with my broth - er _____ in

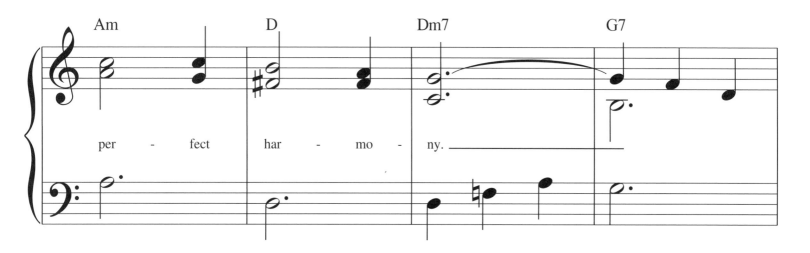

per - fect har - mo - ny. _____

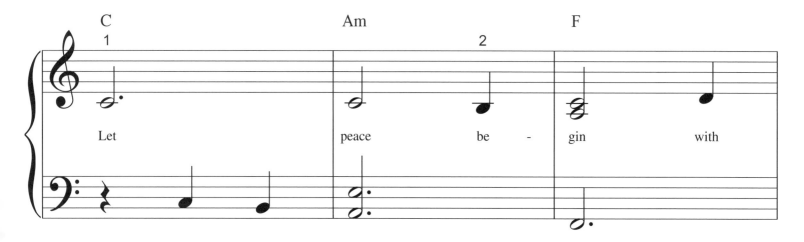

Let peace be - gin with

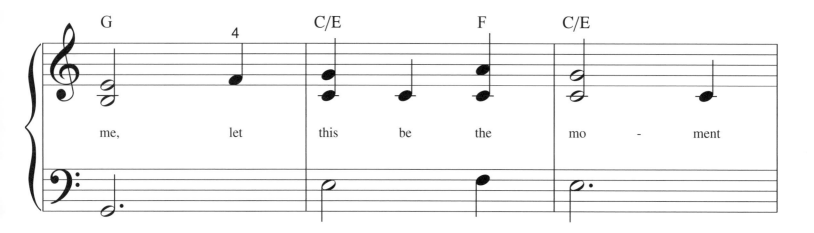

me, let this be the mo - ment

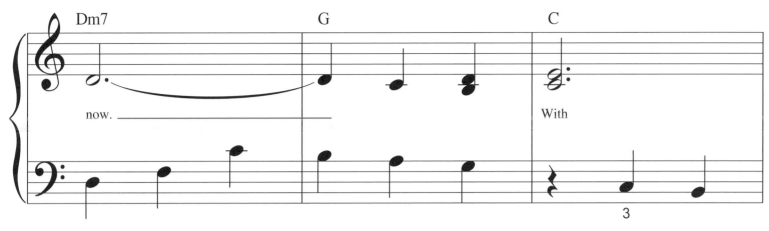

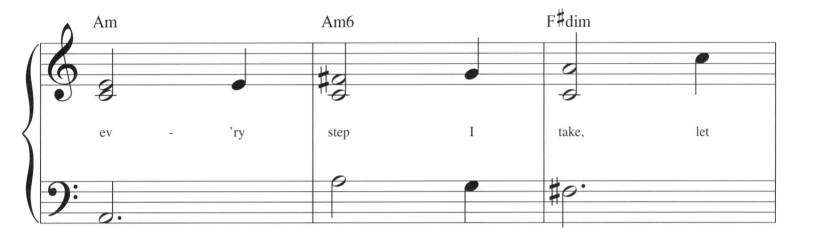

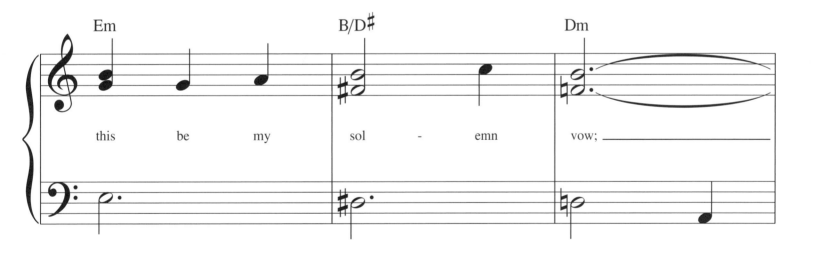

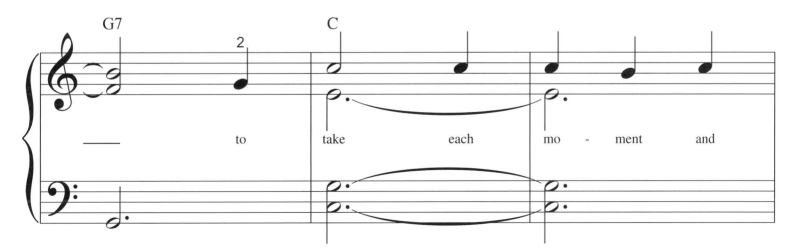

live   each   mo - ment   in   peace   e -

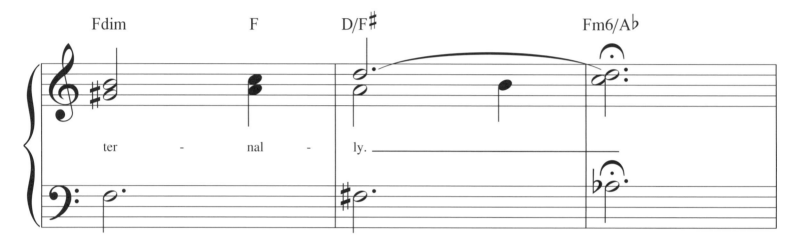

ter   -   nal   -   ly.

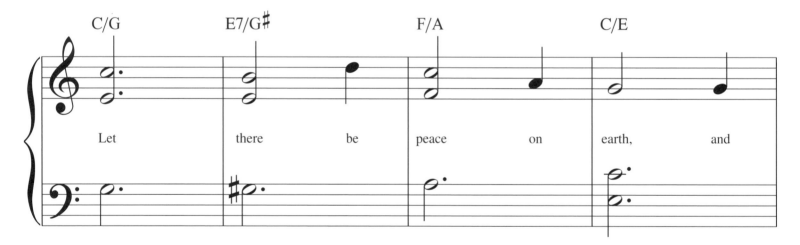

Let   there   be   peace   on   earth,   and

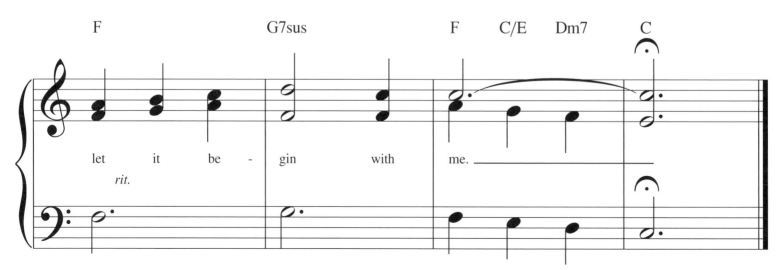

let   it   be - gin   with   me.

rit.

ONE MOMENT IN TIME

Words and Music by ALBERT HAMMOND
and JOHN BETTIS

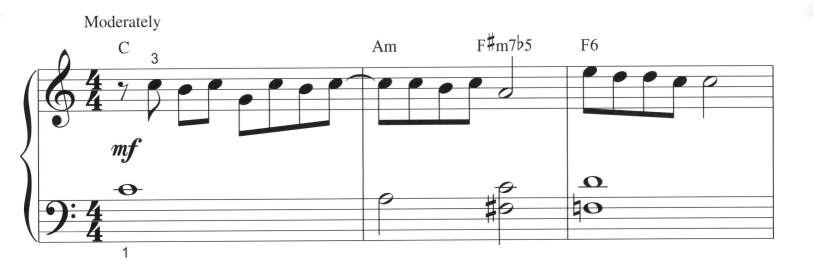

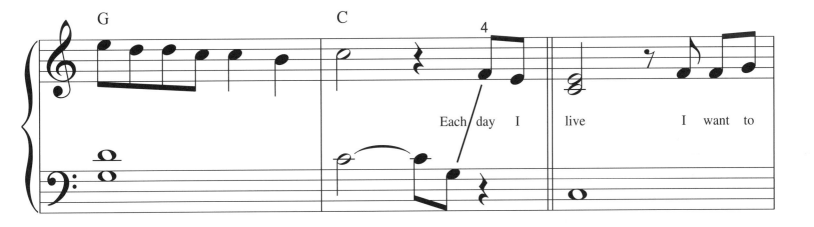

Each day I live I want to

be a day to give the best of me. I'm on-ly

Copyright © 1988 by ALBERT HAMMOND MUSIC and JOHN BETTIS MUSIC
All Rights for ALBERT HAMMOND MUSIC Administered by BMG RIGHTS MANAGEMENT (US) LLC
All Rights for JOHN BETTIS MUSIC Administered by WB MUSIC CORP.
All Rights Reserved   Used by Permission

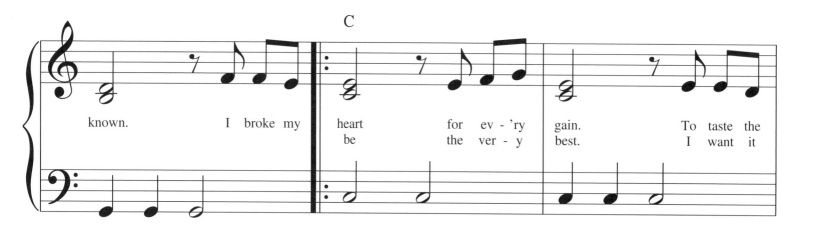

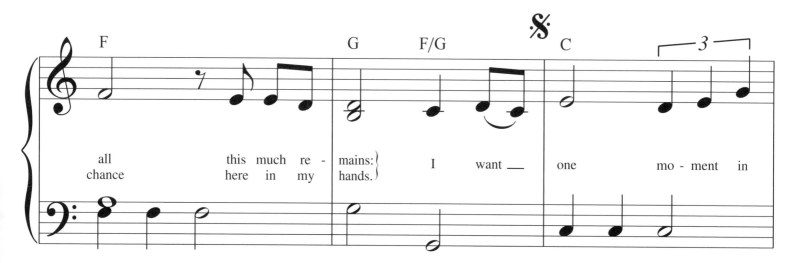

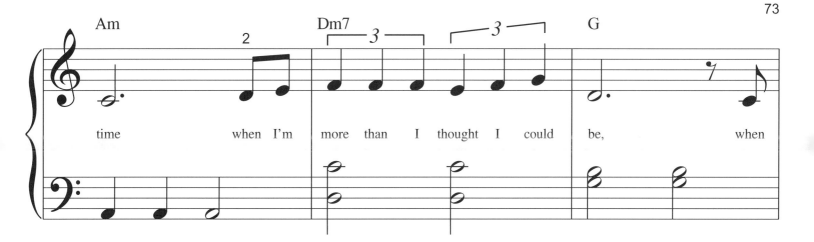

time   when I'm   more than I thought I could   be,   when

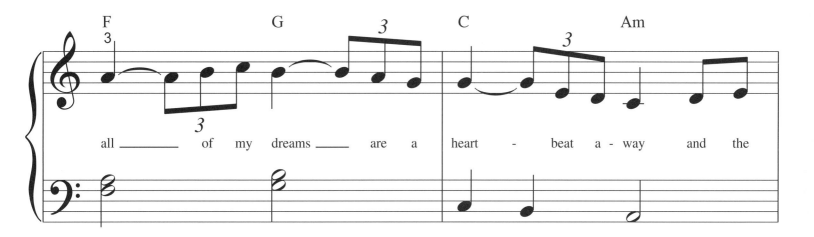

all ____ of my dreams ____ are a   heart - beat a - way   and the

an - swers are all up to   me.   Give me ____ one   mo - ment in

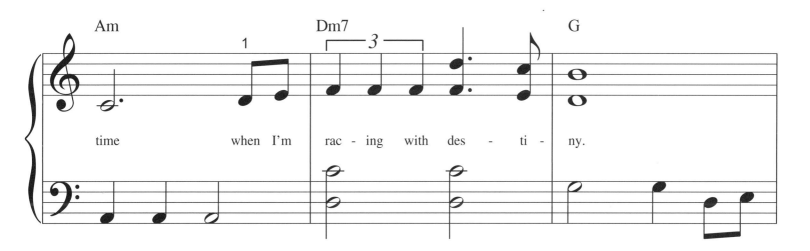

time   when I'm   rac - ing with des - ti - ny.

74

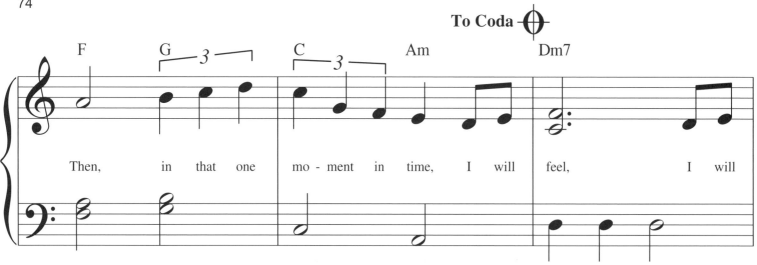

Then, in that one mo - ment in time, I will feel, I will

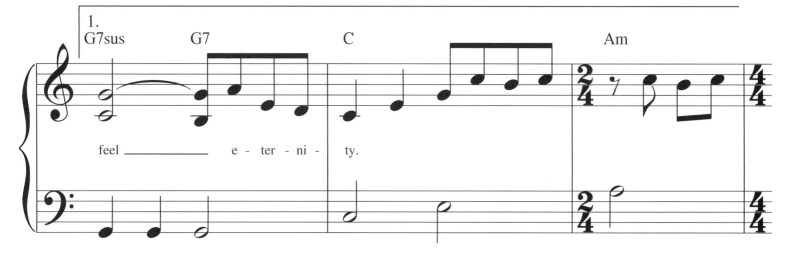

feel _____ e - ter - ni - ty.

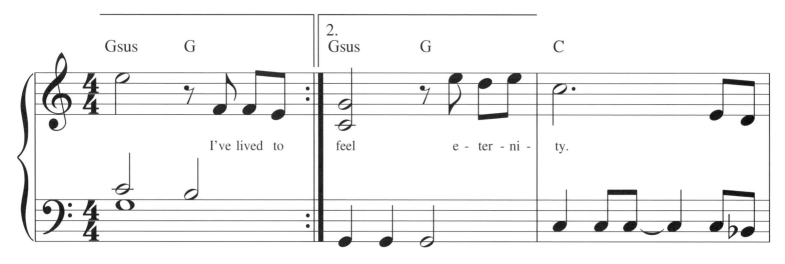

I've lived to feel e - ter - ni - ty.

You're a win - ner for a life - time

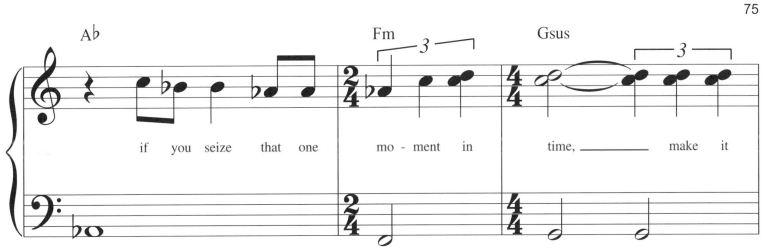

if you seize that one mo - ment in time, _____ make it

D.S. al Coda

shine. Give me

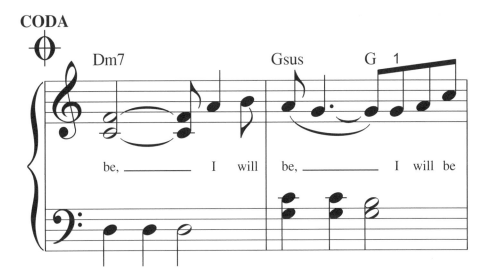

CODA

be, _____ I will be, _____ I will be

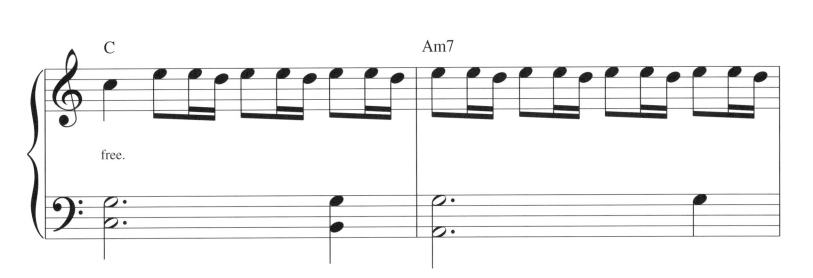

free.

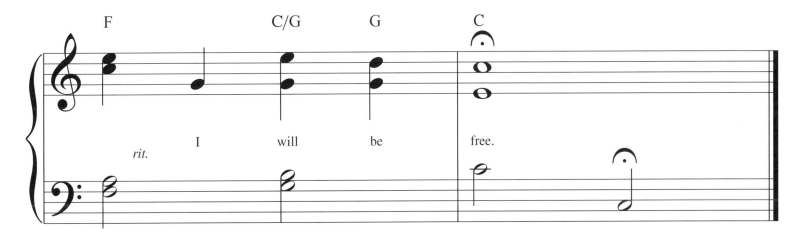

rit. I will be free.

ON EAGLE'S WINGS

Words and Music by
MICHAEL JONCAS

© 1979 Jan Michael Joncas
Published by OCP, 5536 NE Hassalo, Portland, OR 97213
All Rights Reserved   Used by Permission

make you to shine ___ like the sun,   and   hold you in ___ the ___

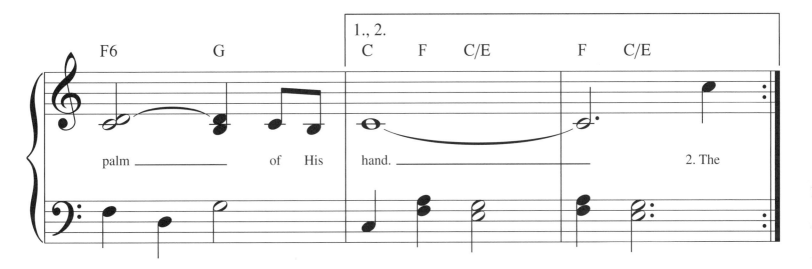

palm ___ of His hand. ___   2. The

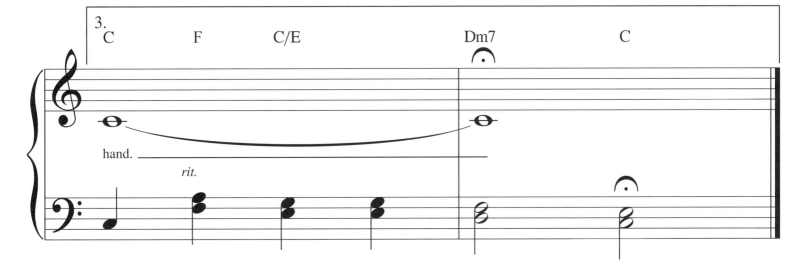

hand. ___
rit.

Additional Lyrics

2. The snare of the fowler will never capture you,
   And famine will bring you no fear:
   Under His wings your refuge,
   His faithfulness your shield.
   Refrain

3. For to the angels He's given a command
   To guard you in all of your ways;
   Upon their hands they will bear you up,
   Lest you dash your foot against a stone.
   Refrain

OVER THE RAINBOW
from THE WIZARD OF OZ

Music by HAROLD ARLEN
Lyric by E.Y. "YIP" HARBURG

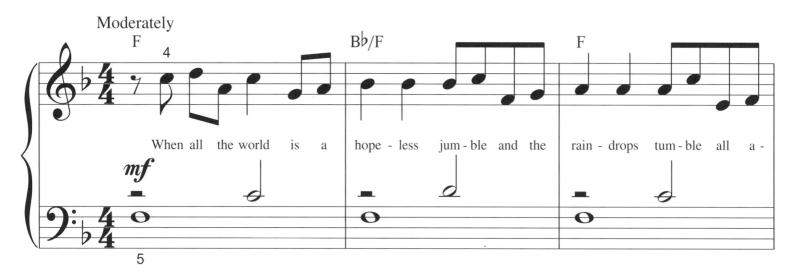

When all the world is a hope-less jum-ble and the rain-drops tum-ble all a-

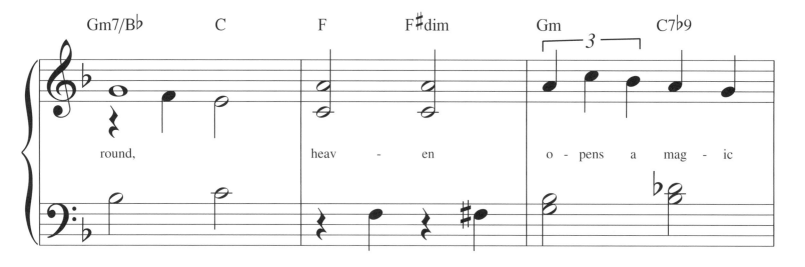

round, heav - en o - pens a mag - ic

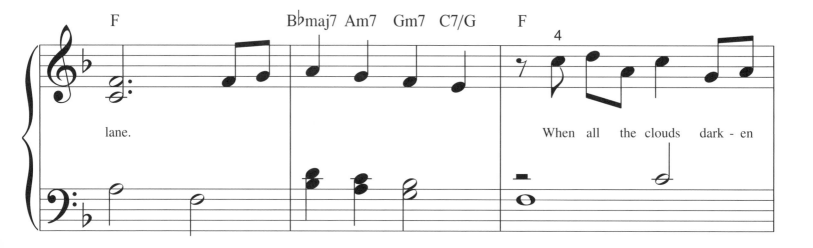

lane. When all the clouds dark - en

© 1938 (Renewed) METRO-GOLDWYN-MAYER INC.
© 1939 (Renewed) EMI FEIST CATALOG INC.
All Rights Administered by EMI FEIST CATALOG INC. (Publishing) and ALFRED MUSIC (Print)
All Rights Reserved   Used by Permission

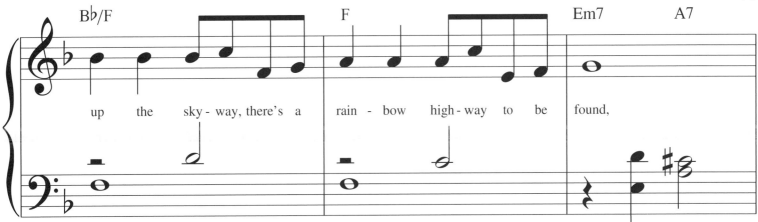

up the sky - way, there's a rain - bow high - way to be found,

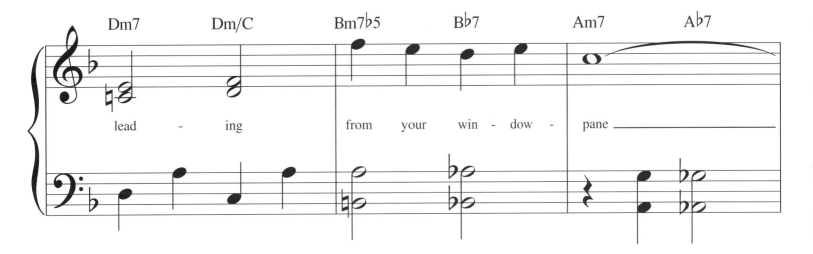

lead - ing from your win - dow - pane _____

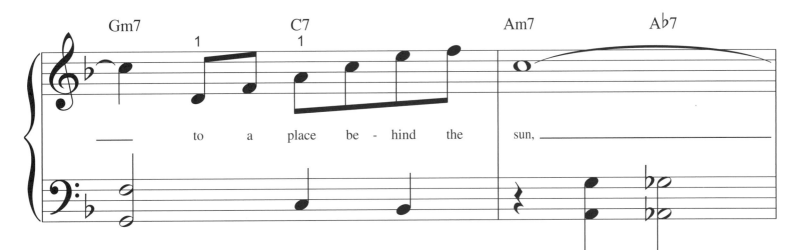

_____ to a place be - hind the sun, _____

just a step be - yond the rain. _____

rit.

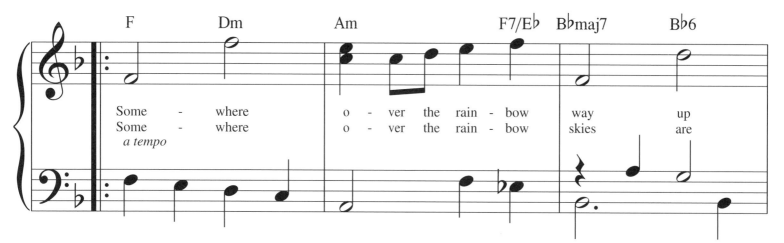

F   Dm   Am   F7/E♭ B♭maj7   B♭6

Some   -   where   o - ver the rain - bow   way   up
Some   -   where   o - ver the rain - bow   skies   are

a tempo

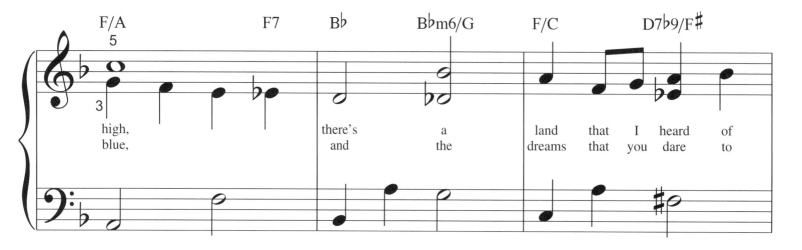

F/A   F7   B♭   B♭m6/G   F/C   D7♭9/F♯

high,   land   that I   heard   of
blue,   there's   a   dreams that you dare   to
          and   the

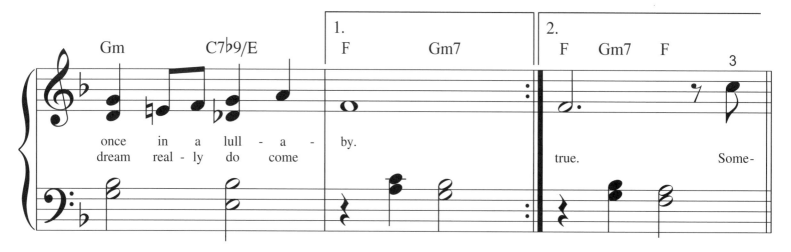

Gm   C7♭9/E   │ 1.   │ 2.
                        │ F   Gm7   │ F   Gm7   F

once   in a lull - a - by.   true.   Some-
dream real - ly do come

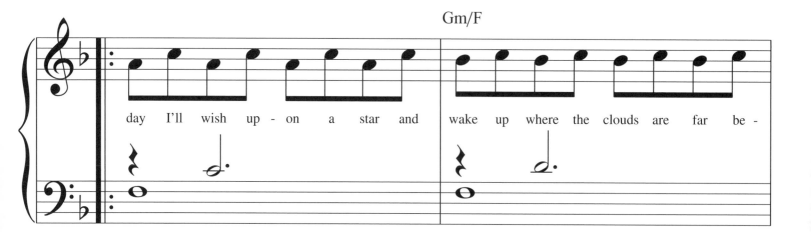

                              Gm/F

day I'll wish up - on a star and   wake up where the clouds are far be -

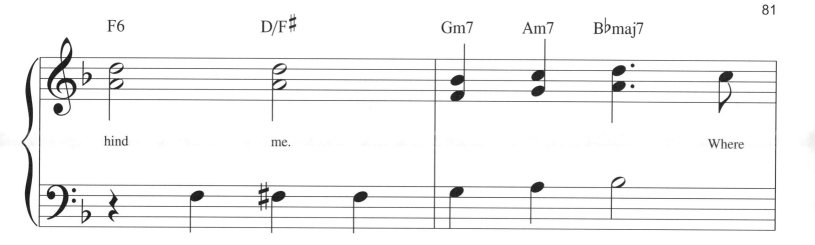

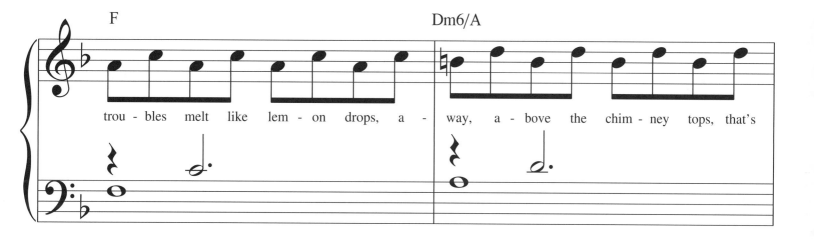

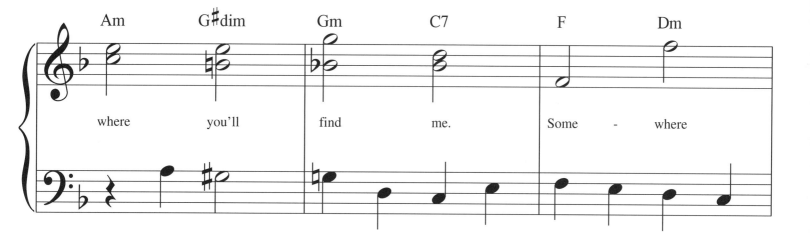

82

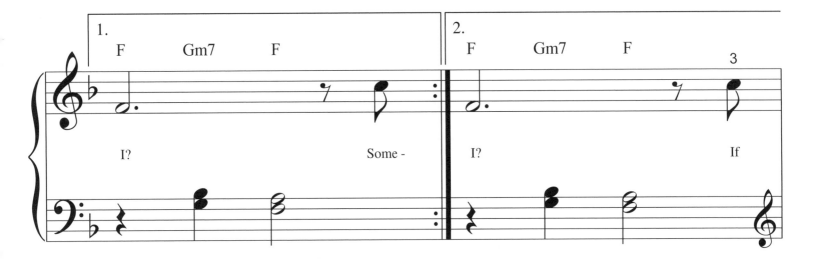

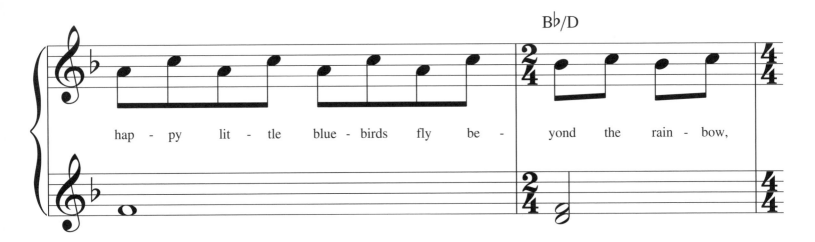

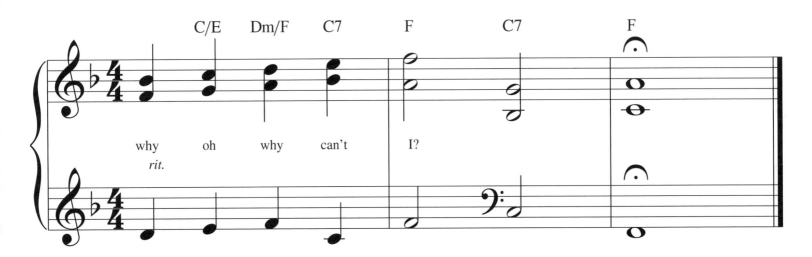

TOUCH THE HAND OF LOVE

Words by MAHRIAH BLACKWOLF,
Music by BLOSSOM DEARIE

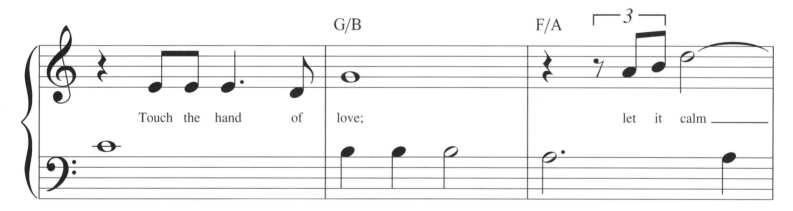

Touch the hand of love; let it calm

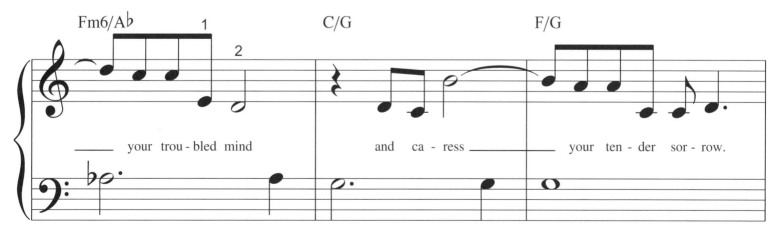

your trou-bled mind and ca-ress your ten-der sor-row.

Copyright © 1981 by BLOSSOM DEARIE MUSIC
All Rights Reserved   Used by Permission

Know ___ the hand of love ___ as you walk ___ that wea - ry

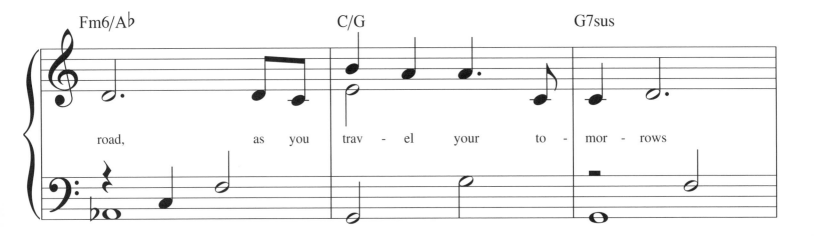

road, ___ as you trav - el your to - mor - rows

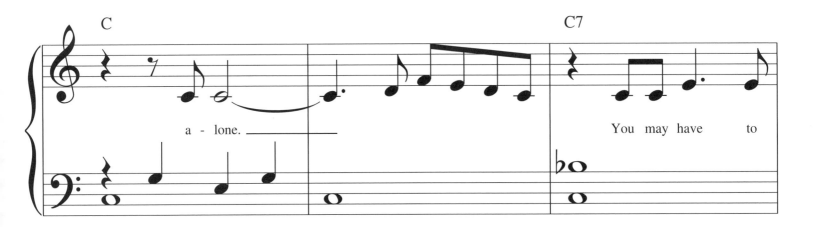

a - lone. ___ You may have to

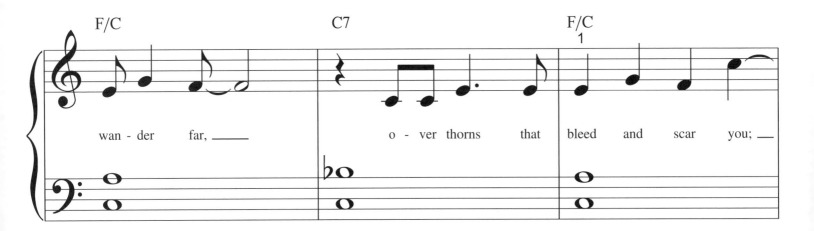

wan - der far, ___ o - ver thorns that bleed and scar you; ___

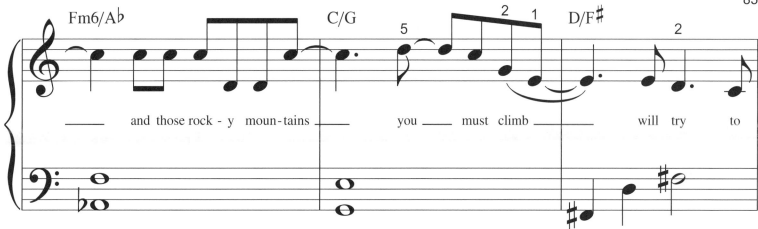

and those rock - y moun-tains _____ you _____ must climb _____ will try to

blind you. Touch the hand of love as you

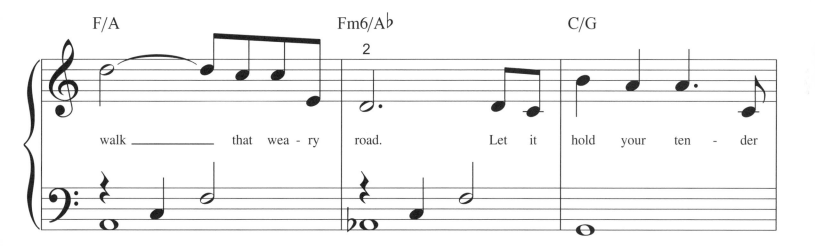

walk _____ that wea - ry road. Let it hold your ten - der

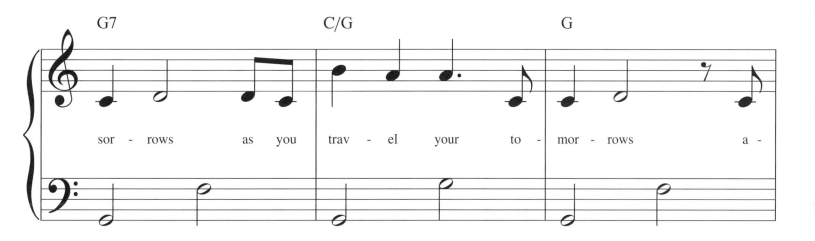

sor - rows as you trav - el your to - mor - rows a -

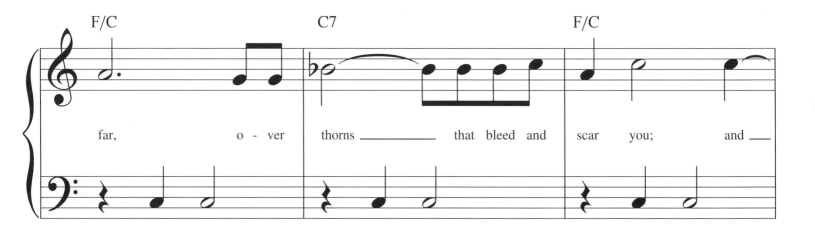

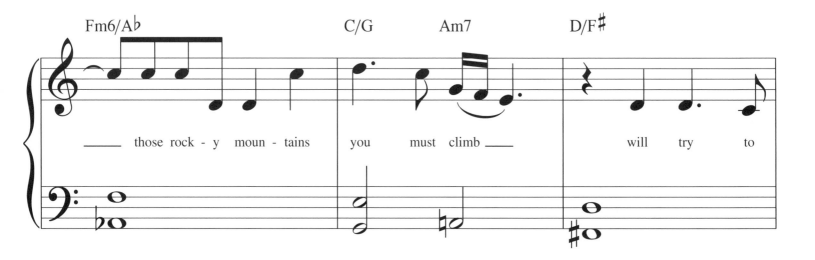

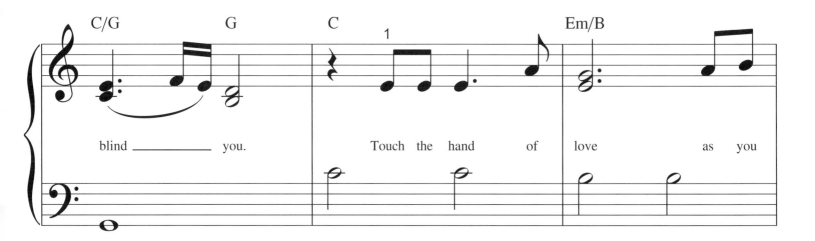

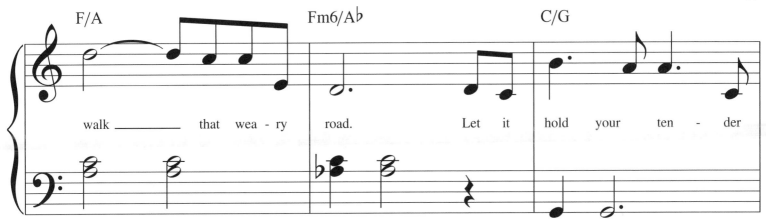

walk _____ that wea - ry road. Let it hold your ten - der

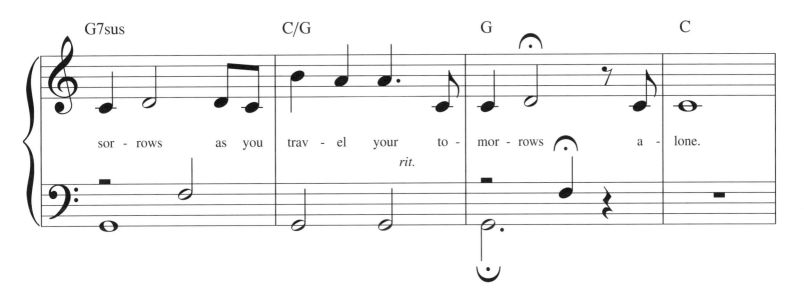

sor - rows as you trav - el your to - mor - rows a - lone.

rit.

a tempo

rit.

PEOPLE GOT TO BE FREE

Words and Music by FELIX CAVALIERE
and EDWARD BRIGATI, JR.

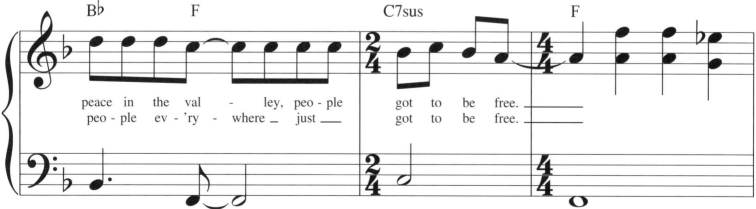

© 1968 (Renewed 1996) EMI JEMAXAL MUSIC INC. and DELICIOUS APPLE MUSIC CORP.
All Rights Reserved   International Copyright Secured   Used by Permission

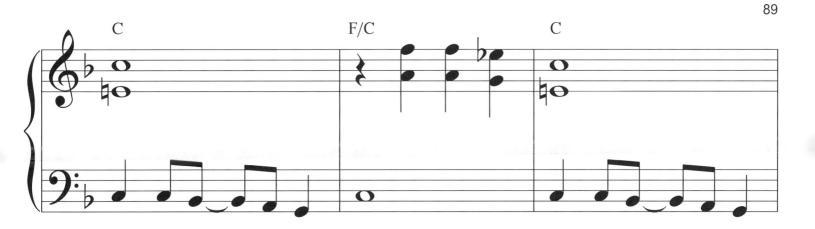

You should see ____ what a love-ly, love-ly world this would
If there's a man who is down and needs a help - ing

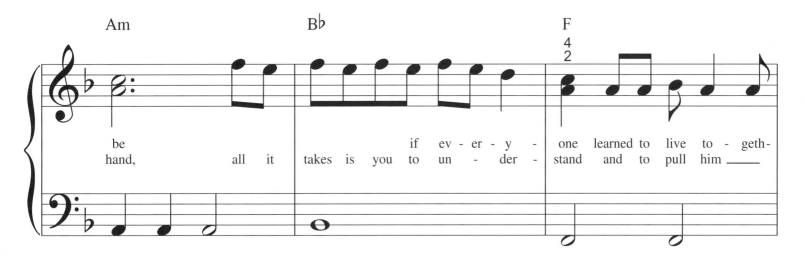

be if ev-er-y - one learned to live to-geth-
hand, all it takes is you to un - der - stand and to pull him ____

er. Seems to me, ___
through. Seems to me, ___

90

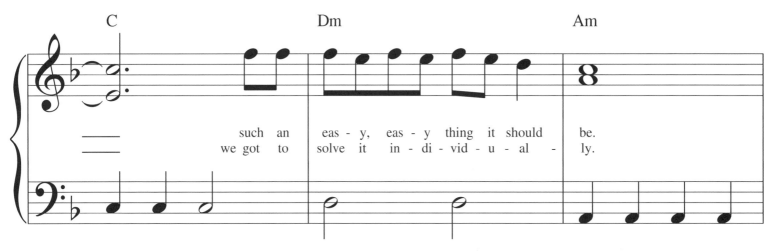

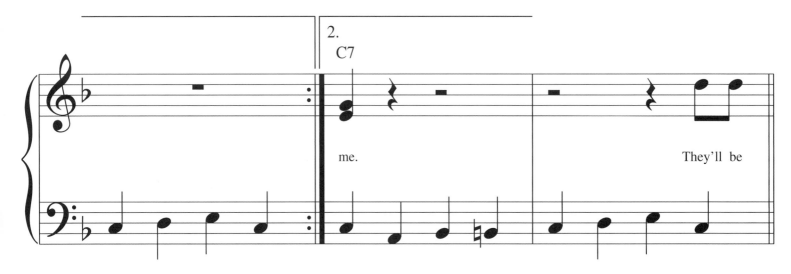

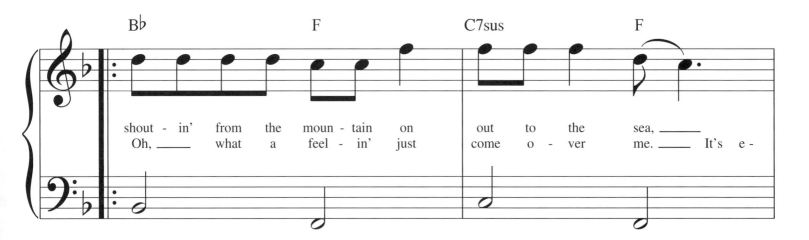

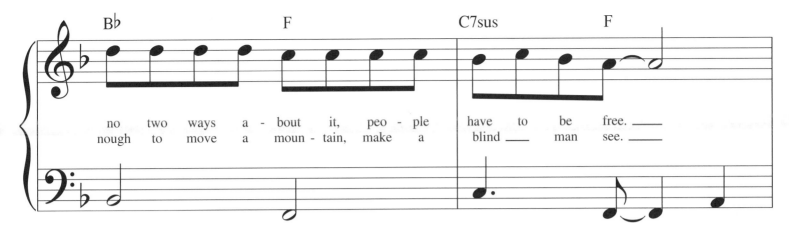

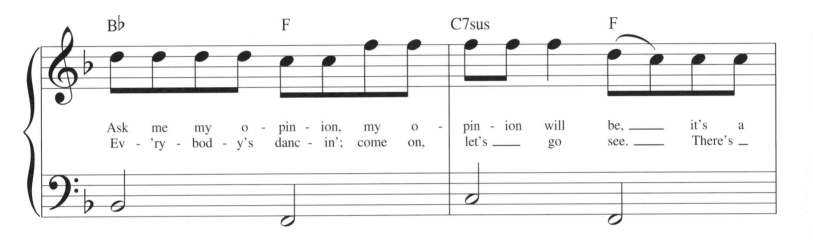

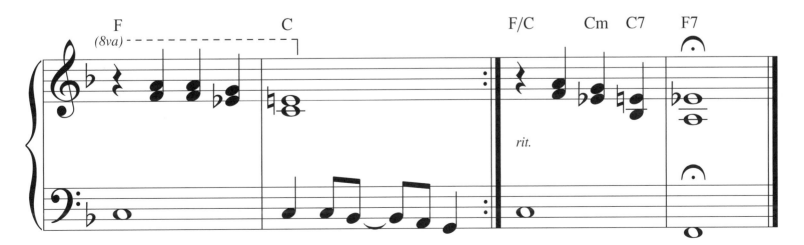

PUT A LITTLE LOVE IN YOUR HEART

Words and Music by JIMMY HOLIDAY,
RANDY MYERS and JACKIE DeSHANNON

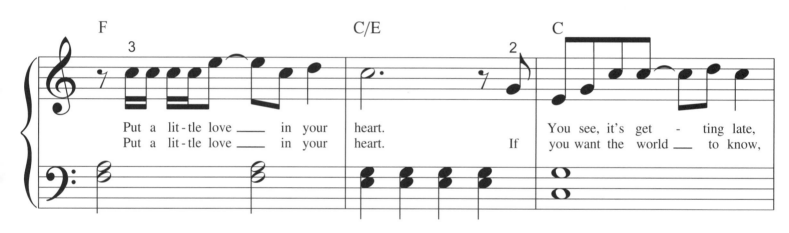

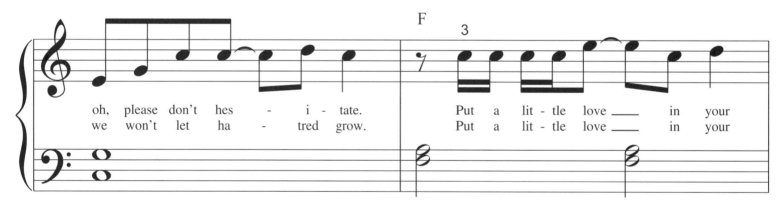

© 1969 (Renewed) EMI UNART CATALOG INC.
All Rights Administered by EMI UNART CATALOG INC. (Publishing) and ALFRED MUSIC (Print)
All Rights Reserved   Used by Permission

world   will be a   bet -ter place   for   you   and

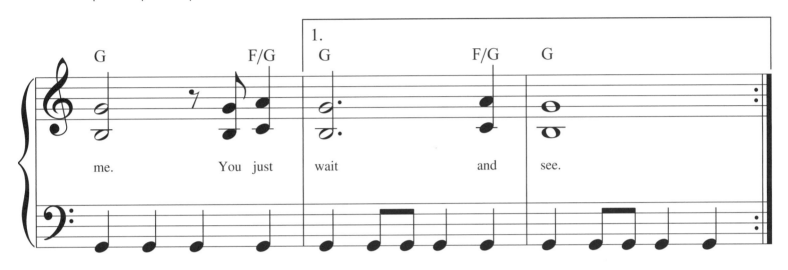

me.   You just   wait   and   see.

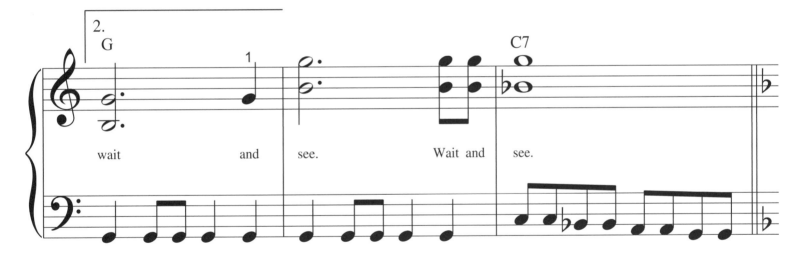

wait   and   see.   Wait and   see.

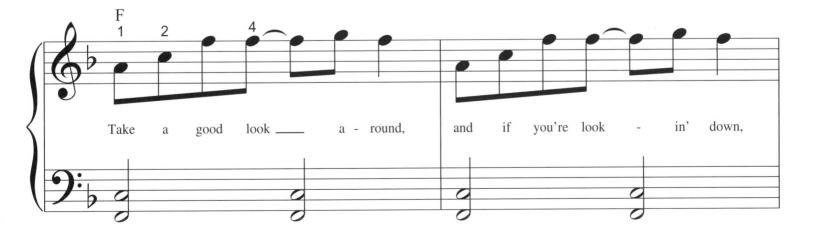

Take a good look   a -round,   and if you're look - in' down,

put a lit-tle love ___ in your heart. I hope when you ___ de - cide,

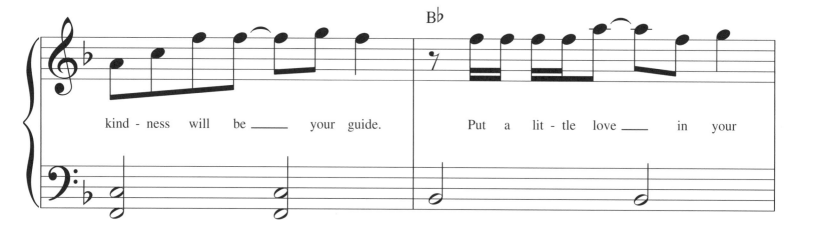

kind - ness will be ___ your guide. Put a lit - tle love ___ in your

heart. ___ And the world will be a bet - ter place. ___ And the

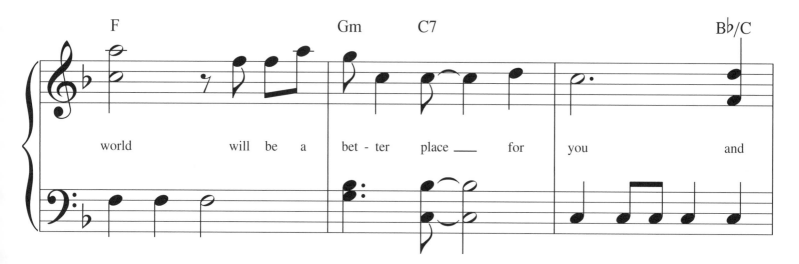

world will be a bet - ter place ___ for you and

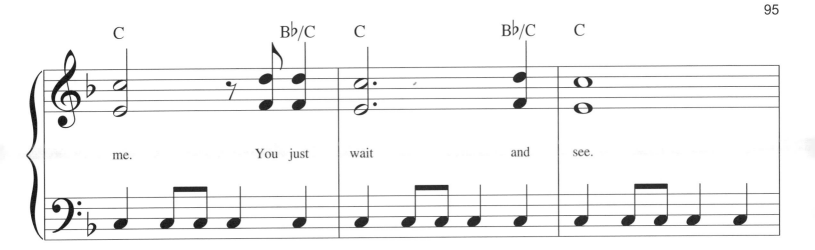

me. You just wait and see.

Put a lit-tle love in your heart. Put a lit-tle love in your

heart. Put a lit-tle love in your heart.

Put a lit-tle love in your heart.

REACH

Words and Music by GLORIA ESTEFAN
and DIANE WARREN

Moderately

Some dreams live
days are

on in time ___ for - ev - er.
meant to be ___ re - mem - bered.

Those dreams, ___ you want with all ___ your heart. ___
Those days ___ we rise a - bove ___ the skies. ___

And I'll do what - ev - er it takes, ___ fol - low
And so I'll go the dis - tance this time, ___ see - ing

© 1995 FOREIGN IMPORTED PRODUCTIONS & PUBLISHING, INC. (BMI) and REALSONGS (ASCAP)
All Rights Reserved   Used by Permission

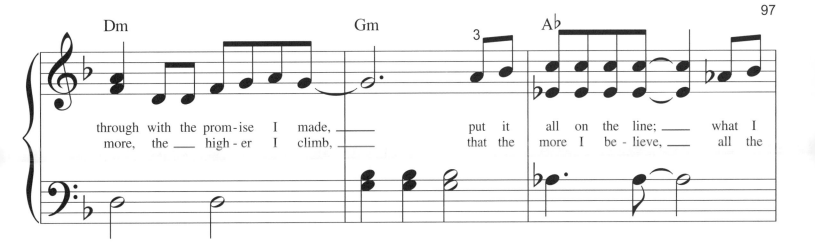

through with the prom-ise I made, _____ put it all on the line; _____ what I
more, the __ high - er I climb, _____ that the more I be - lieve, _____ all the

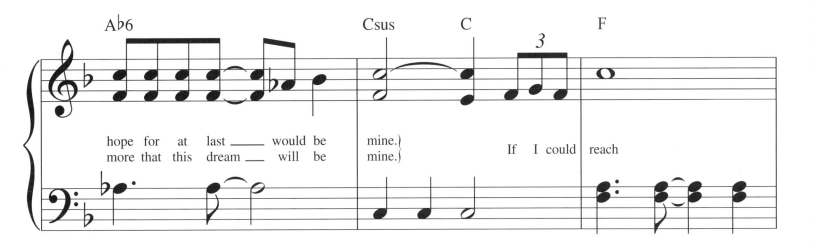

hope for at last _____ would be mine.) If I could reach
more that this dream __ will be mine.)

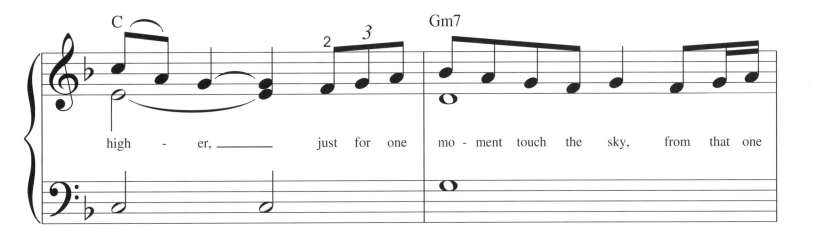

high - er, _____ just for one mo - ment touch the sky, from that one

mo - ment in my life, I'm gon-na be _____ strong - er, _____ know that I've

tried my ver - y best, put my spir - it to the test if I could

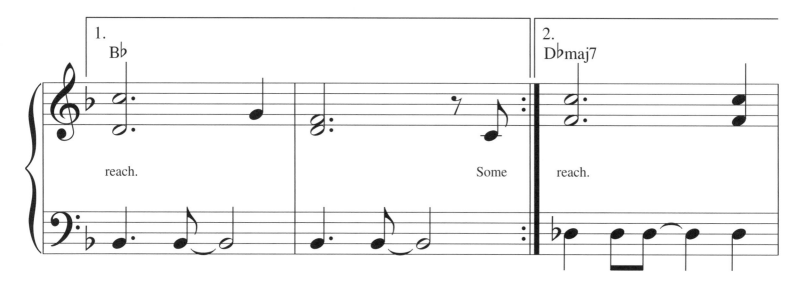

1. reach.

Some

2. reach.

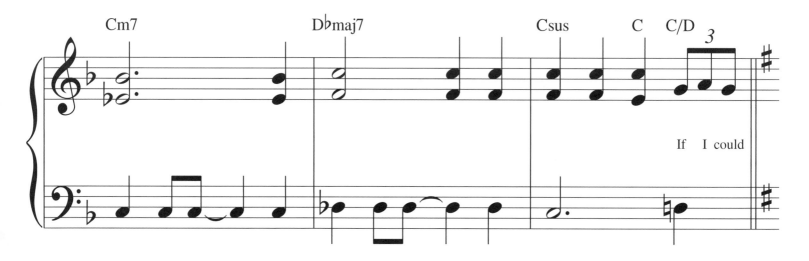

If I could

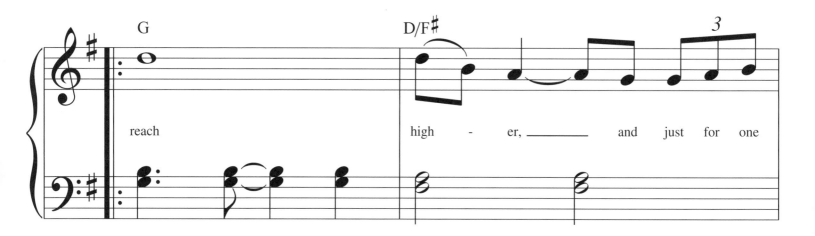

reach high - er, _____ and just for one

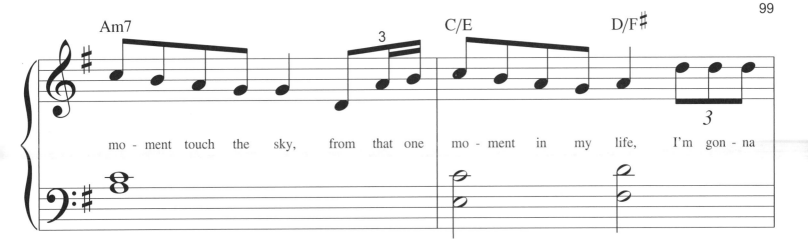

SHOWER THE PEOPLE

Words and Music by
JAMES TAYLOR

You can
play the game ___ and you can
You can run _____ but you

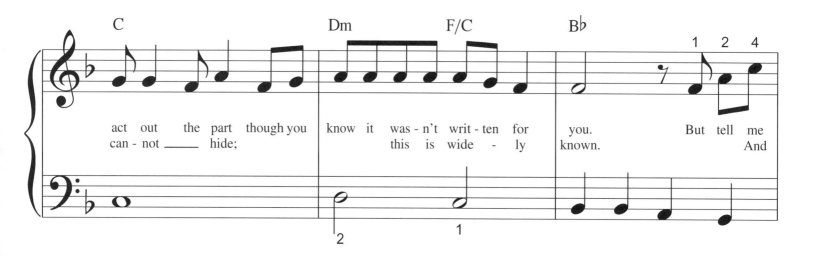

act out the part though you know it was-n't writ-ten for you. But tell me
can-not ___ hide; this is wide - ly known. And

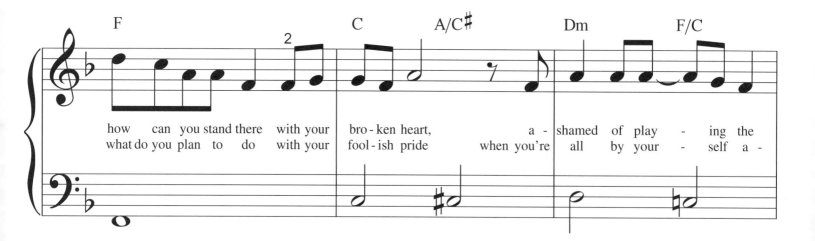

how can you stand there with your bro-ken heart, a-shamed of play - ing the
what do you plan to do with your fool-ish pride when you're all by your - self a-

© 1975 (Renewed) COUNTRY ROAD MUSIC, INC.
All Rights Reserved   Used by Permission

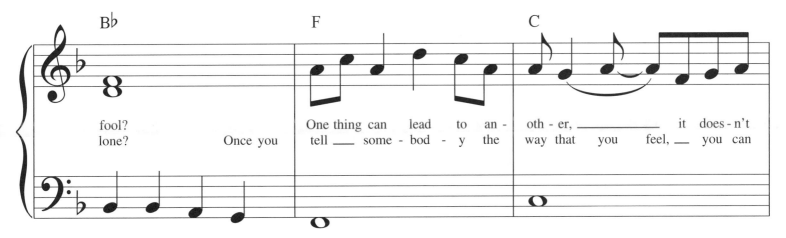

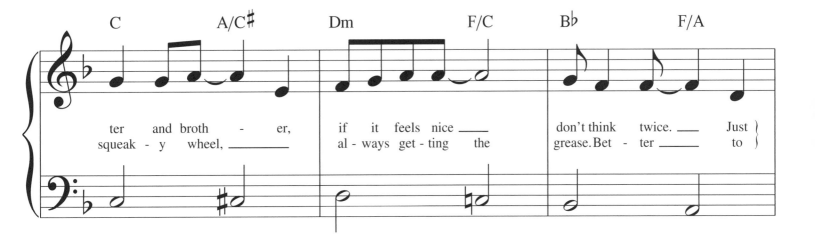

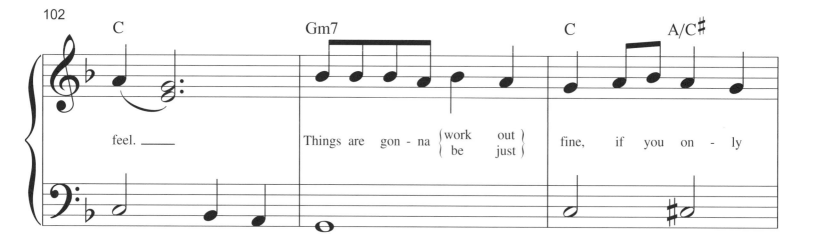

feel. _____ | Things are gon - na {work out / be just} | fine, if you on - ly

will. _____ | What I | mean to say to you, is to | show - er the peo - ple you

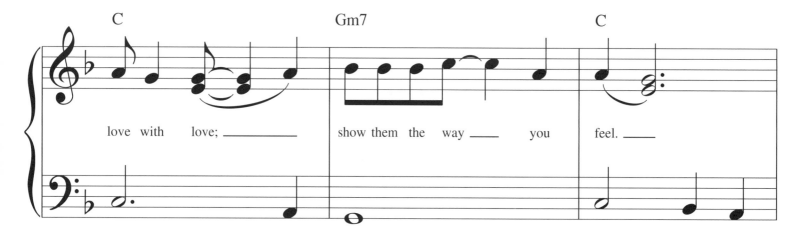

love with love; _____ | show them the way _____ you | feel. _____

Things are gon - na be much | bet - ter if you on - ly

1.
Dm   E♭   B♭   2. Dm

will. _____   will. _____

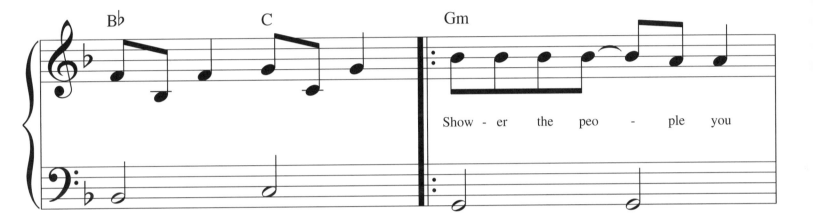

B♭   C   Gm

Show - er the peo - ple you

C   Gm7   1. C

love with love; _____ show them the way ___ you feel. _____

2. C   B♭   Am   Gm7   F

feel. _____   rit.

THAT'S WHAT FRIENDS ARE FOR

Music by BURT BACHARACH
Words by CAROLE BAYER SAGER

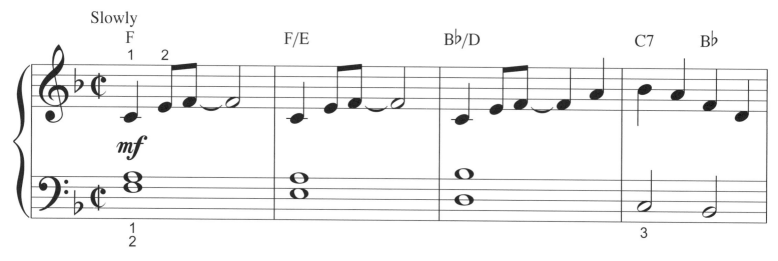

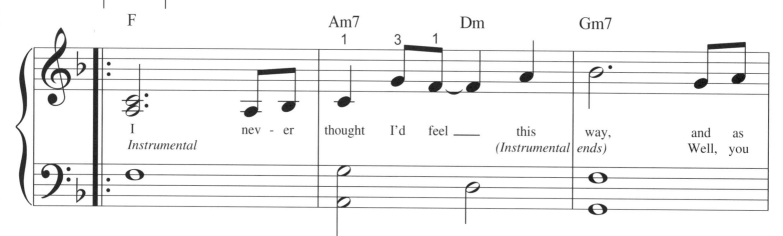

I never thought I'd feel ___ this way, and as
Instrumental (Instrumental ends) Well, you

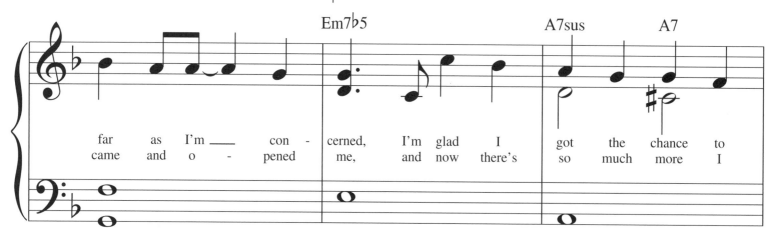

far as's I'm ___ con- cerned, I'm glad I got the chance to
came and o - pened me, and now there's so much more I

© 1982 WB MUSIC CORP., NEW HIDDEN VALLEY MUSIC, WARNER-TAMERLANE PUBLISHING CORP. and CAROLE BAYER SAGER MUSIC
All Rights Administered Jointly by WB MUSIC CORP. and WARNER-TAMERLANE PUBLISHING CORP.
All Rights Reserved   Used by Permission

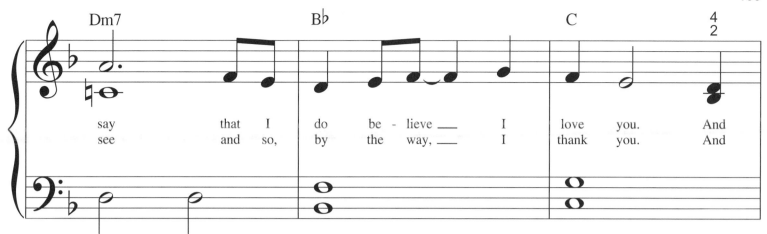

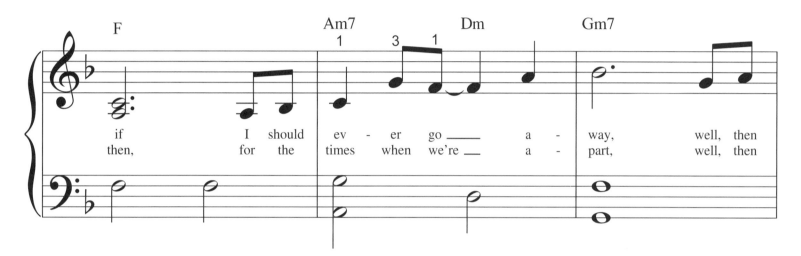

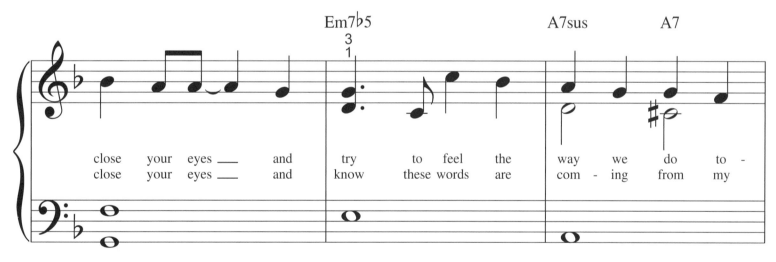

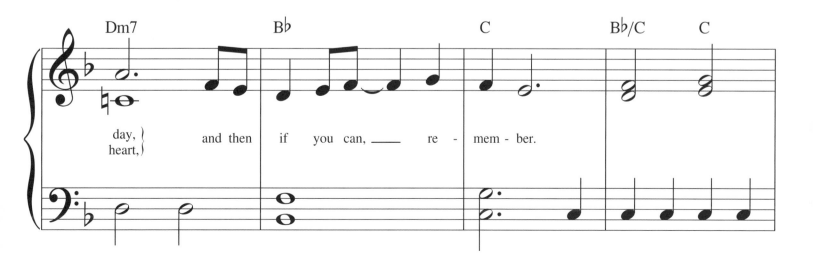

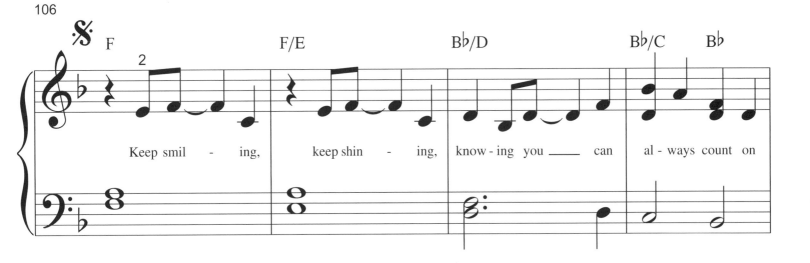

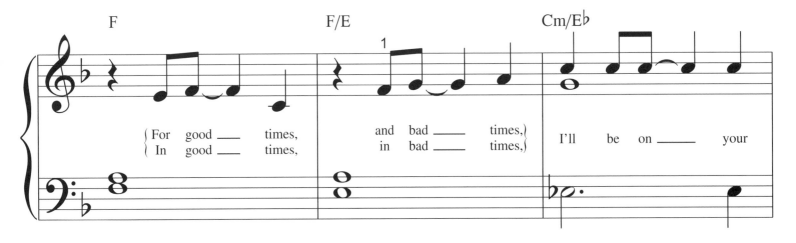

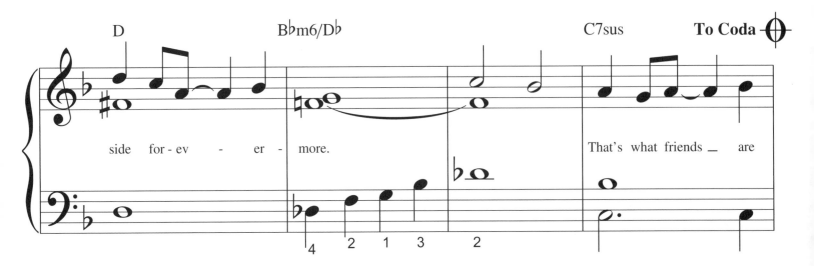

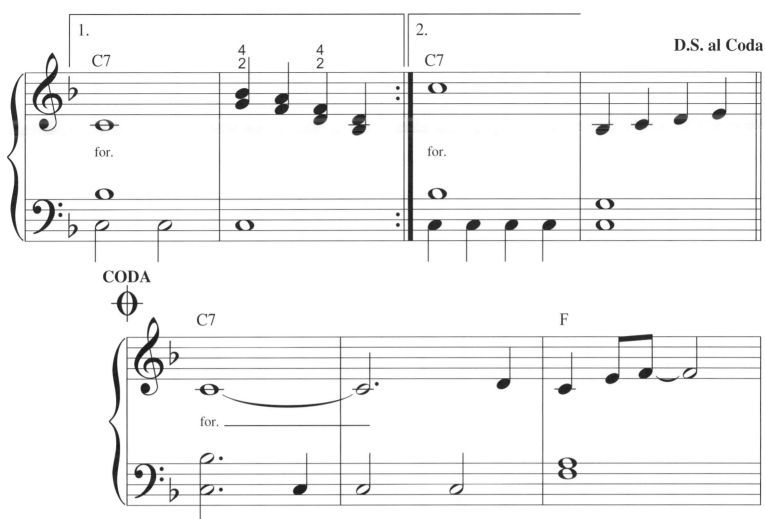

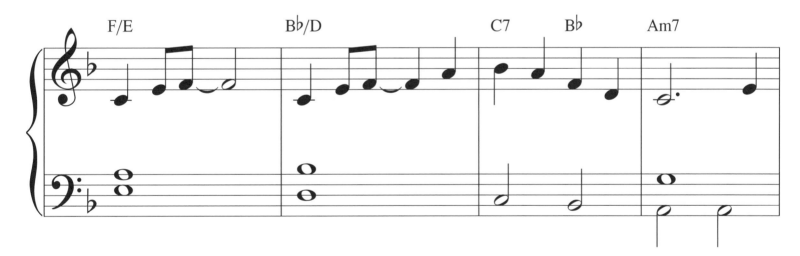

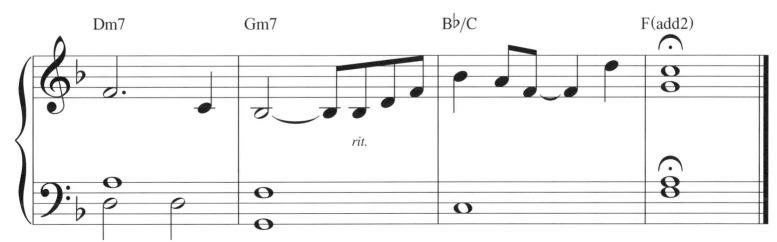

WALKING ON SUNSHINE

Words and Music by
KIMBERLEY REW

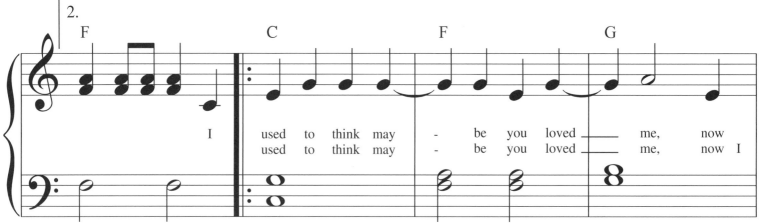

I
used to think may - be you loved ___ me, now
used to think may - be you loved ___ me, now I

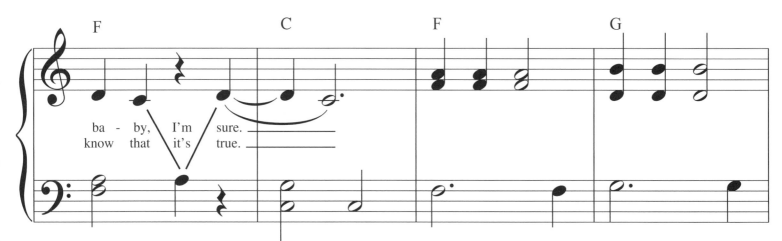

ba - by, I'm sure. ___
know that it's true. ___

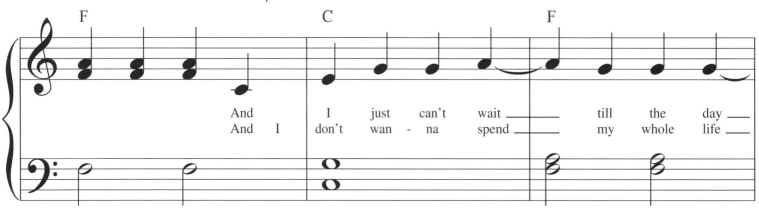

And I just can't wait ___ till the day ___
And I don't wan - na spend ___ my whole life ___

Copyright © 1985 Kyboside Ltd.
Administered in the United States and Canada by Wixen Music Publishing, Inc. as agent for Primary Wave Brian (Kyboside Sp. Acct.)
All Rights Reserved   Used by Permission

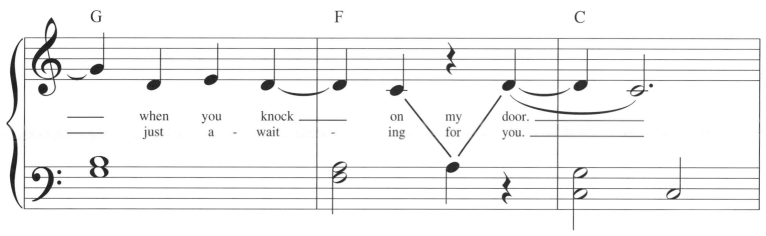

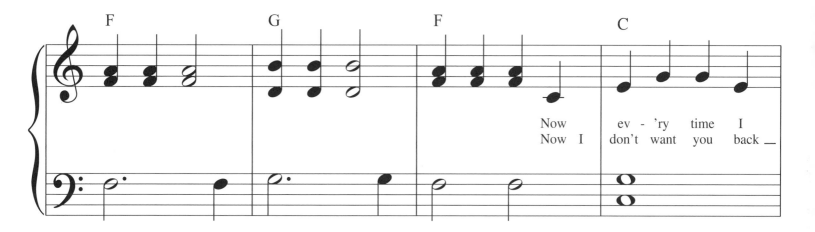

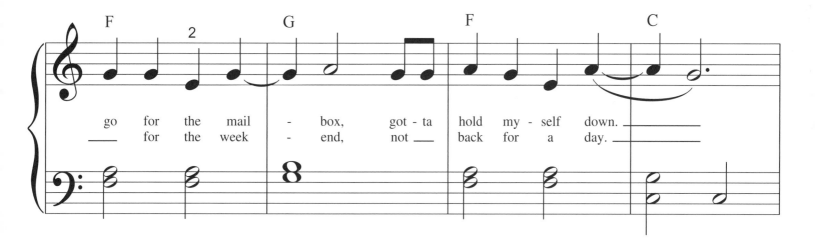

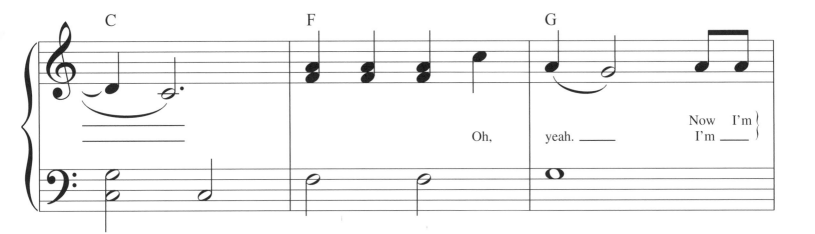

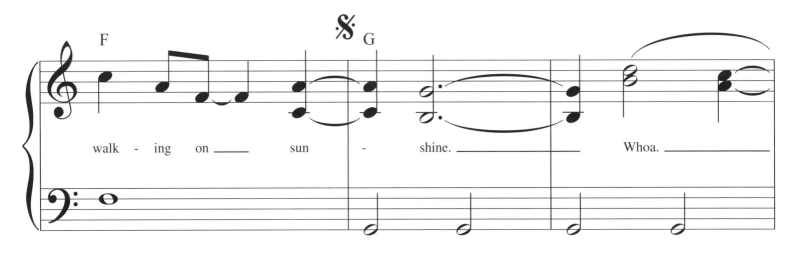

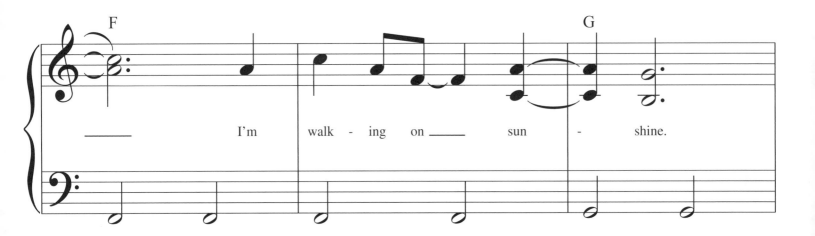

Whoa. _____ I'm walk - ing on _____ sun - shine.

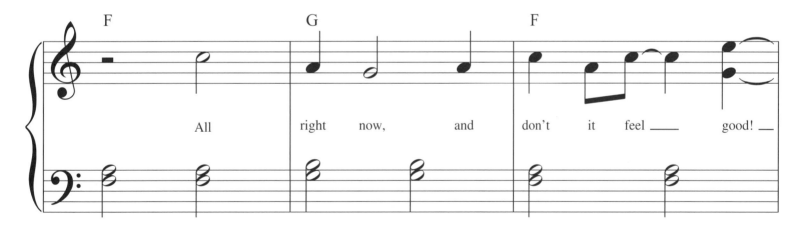

To Coda

Whoa, _____ and don't it feel ____ good! ____

All right now, and don't it feel ____ good! ____

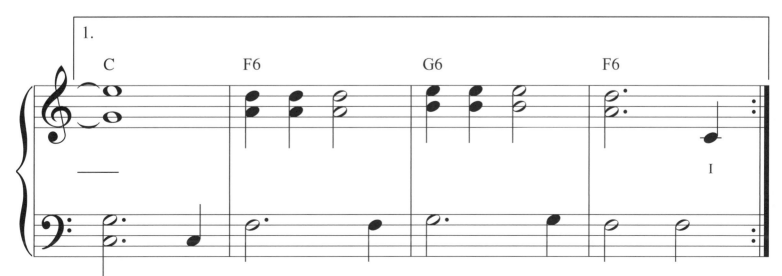

1.

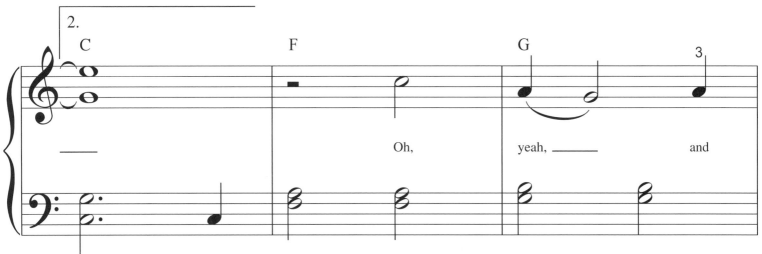

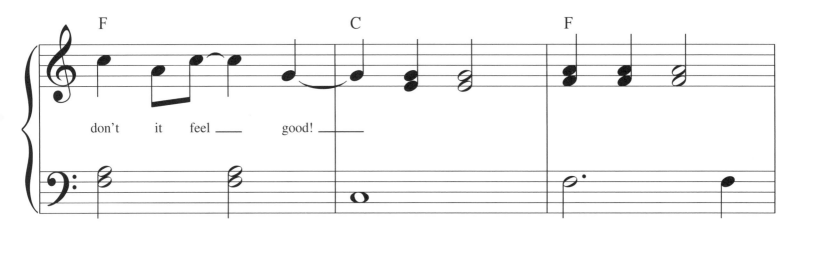

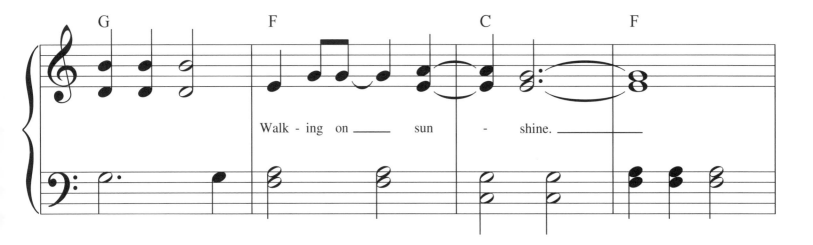

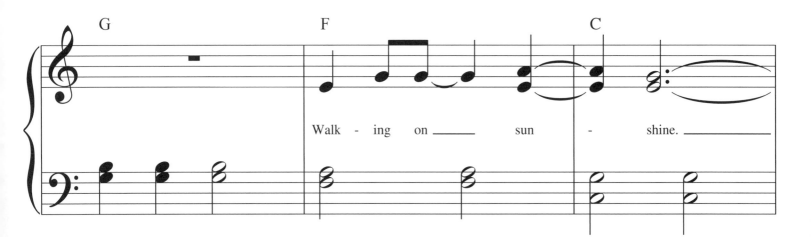

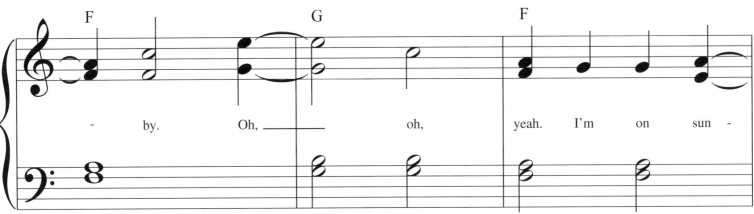

- by. Oh, _____ oh, yeah. I'm on sun -

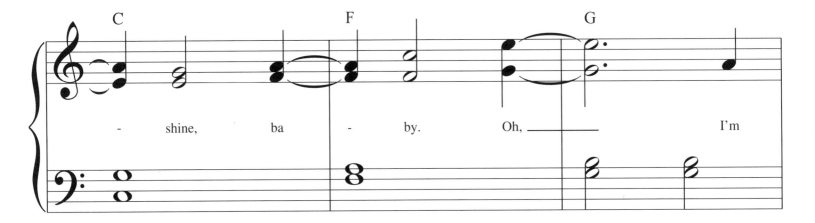

- shine, ba - by. Oh, _____ I'm

walk - ing on _____ sun -

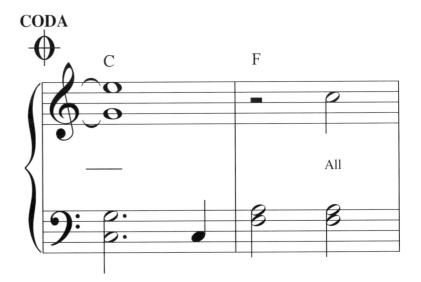

D.S. al Coda

CODA

_____ All

right now, and don't it feel good! _____

WE ARE THE WORLD

Words and Music by LIONEL RICHIE
and MICHAEL JACKSON

Copyright © 1985 by Brockman Music, Brenda Richie Publishing, Warner-Tamerlane Publishing Corp. and Mijac Music
All Rights on behalf of Mijac Music Administered by Sony/ATV Music Publishing LLC, 8 Music Square West, Nashville, TN 37203
All Rights Reserved   Used by Permission

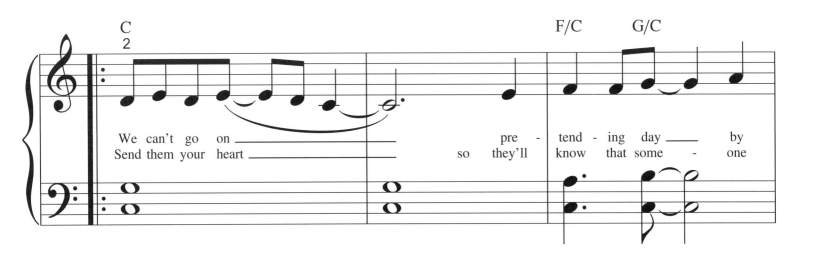

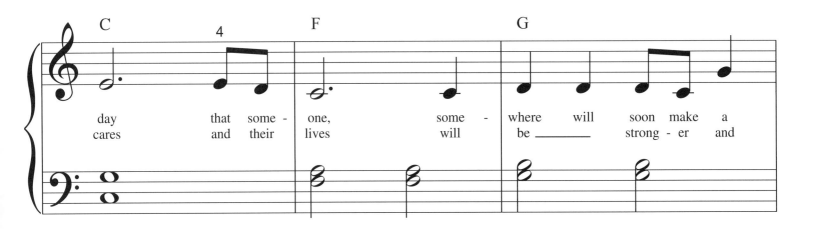

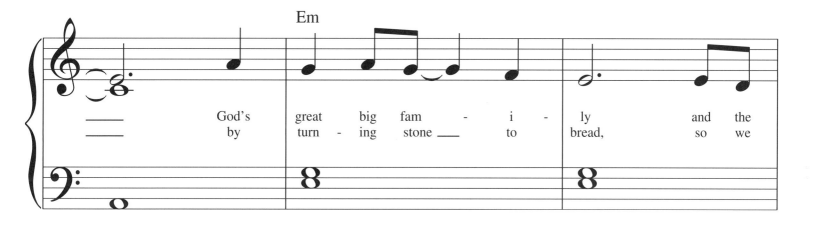

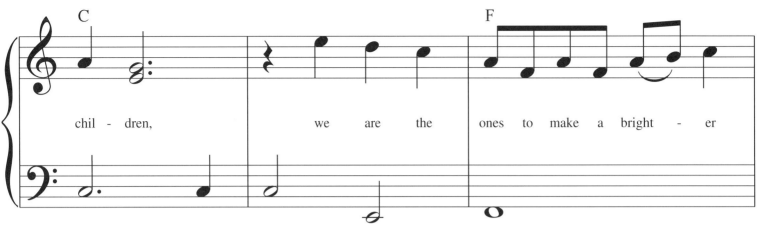

chil - dren, we are the ones to make a bright - er

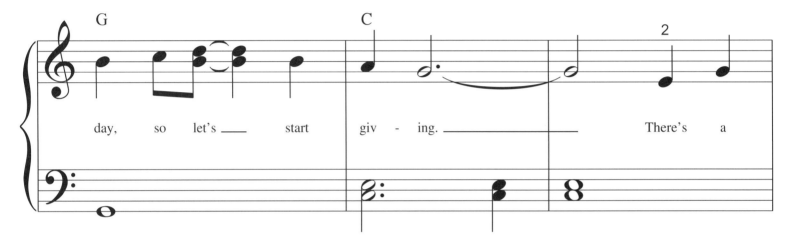

day, so let's ___ start giv - ing. _____ There's a

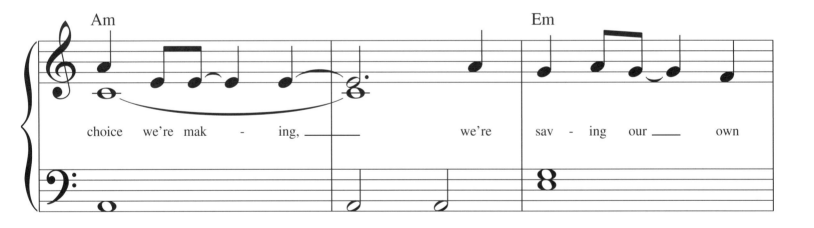

choice we're mak - ing, _____ we're sav - ing our ___ own

To Coda ⊕

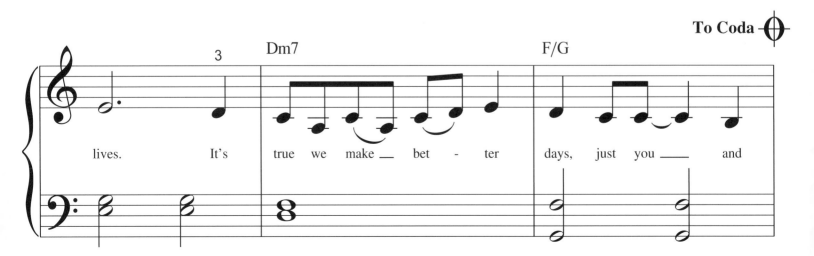

lives. It's true we make __ bet - ter days, just you ___ and

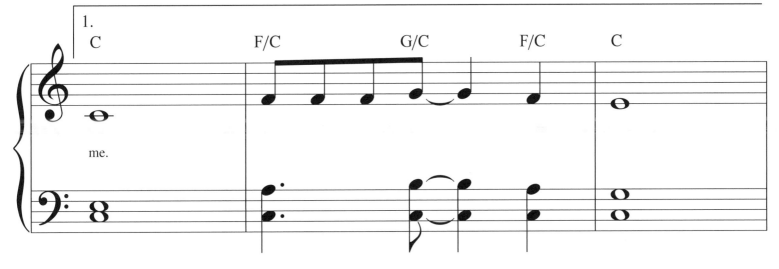

me.

me. ____ When you're

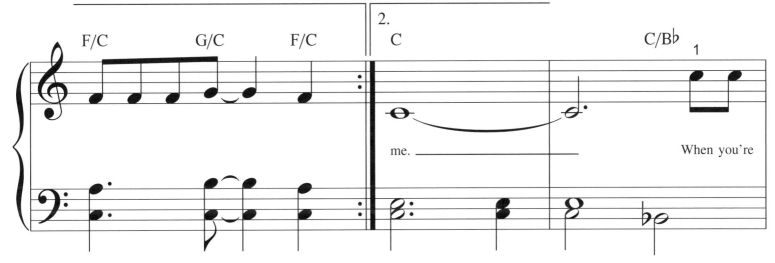

down and out, ____ there seems no hope ____ at all, _____

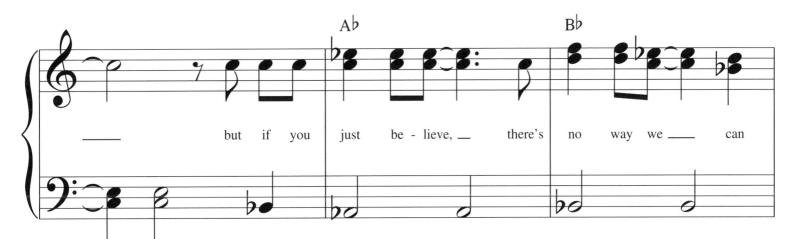

____ but if you just be - lieve, ____ there's no way we ____ can

fall. _____ Let us re - al - ize _____

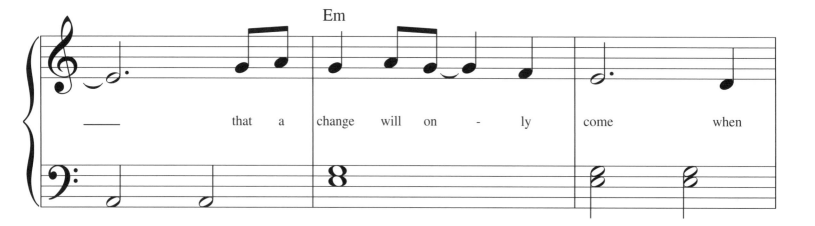

____ that a change will on - ly come when

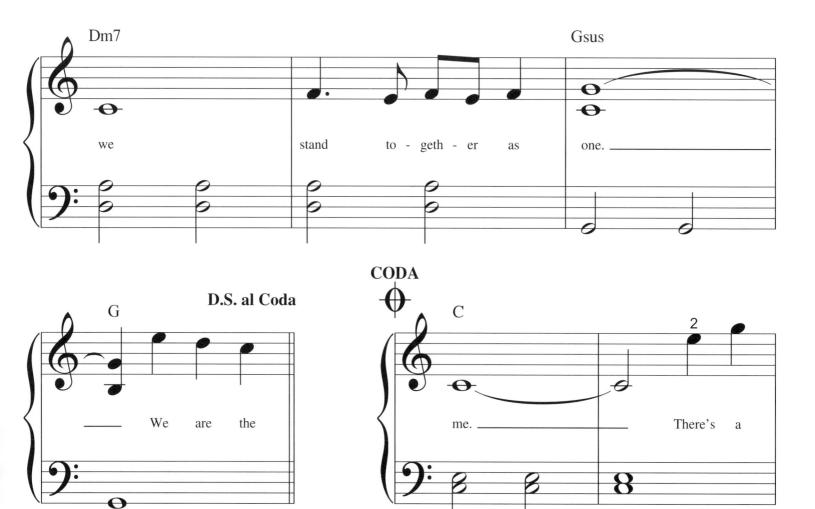

we stand to - geth - er as one. _____

D.S. al Coda

CODA

____ We are the

me. _____ There's a

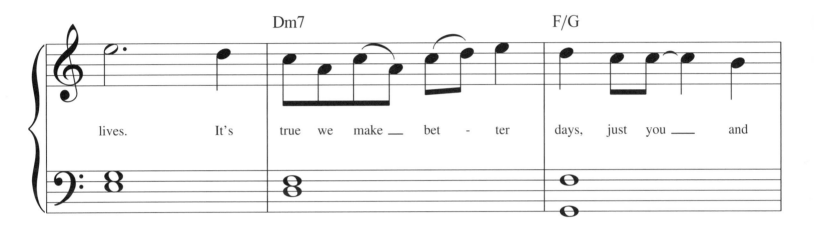

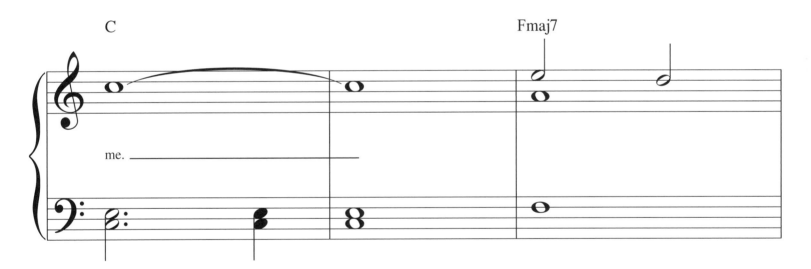

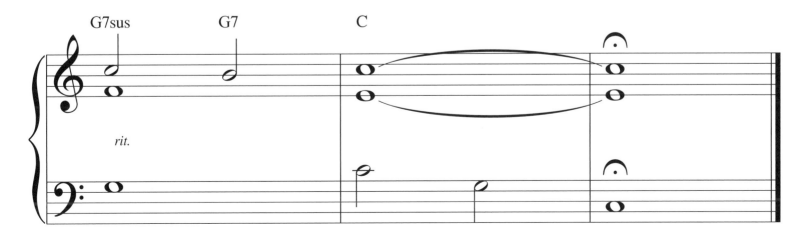

WE ARE THE CHAMPIONS

Words and Music by
FREDDIE MERCURY

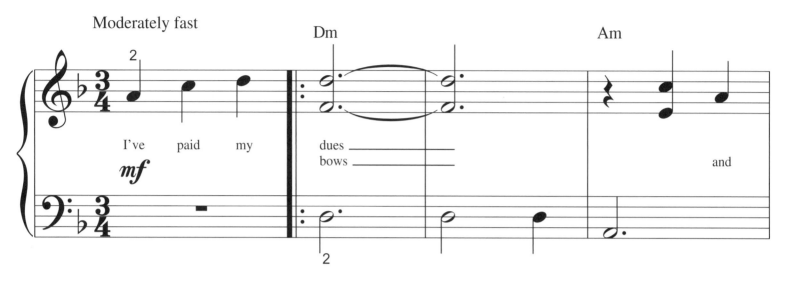

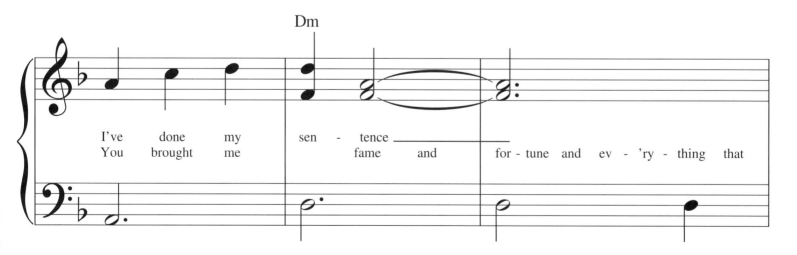

© 1977 (Renewed 2005) QUEEN MUSIC LTD.
All Rights for the U.S. and Canada Controlled and Administered by BEECHWOOD MUSIC CORP.
All Rights for the world excluding the U.S. and Canada Controlled and Administered by EMI MUSIC PUBLISHING LTD.
All Rights Reserved   International Copyright Secured   Used by Permission

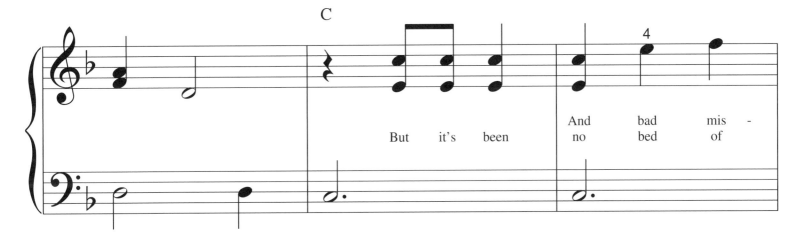

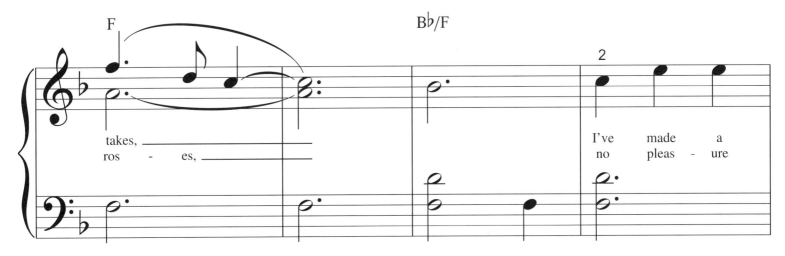

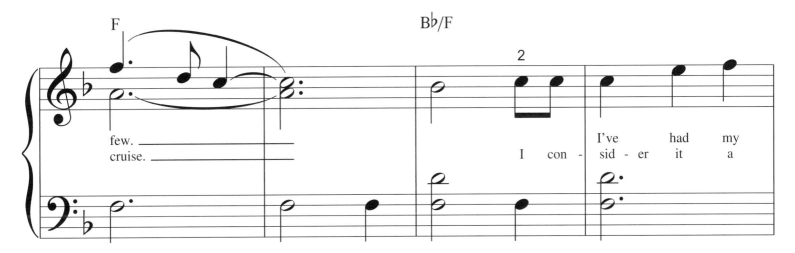

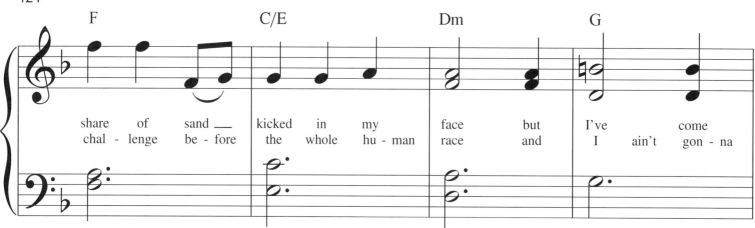

F   C/E   Dm   G

share of sand ___ kicked in my face but I've come
chal - lenge be - fore the whole hu - man race and I ain't gon - na

C   C9

through. }
lose. }
And I need to go on, and on, and

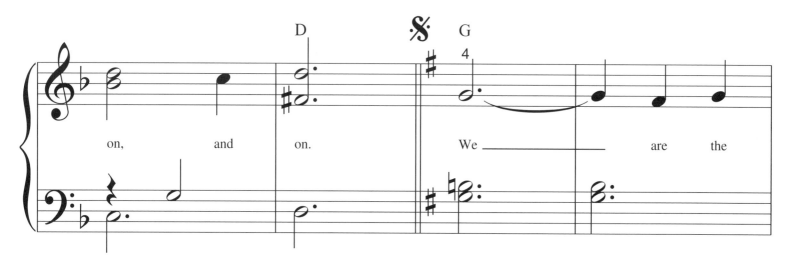

D   𝄋   G

on, and on. We ___ are the

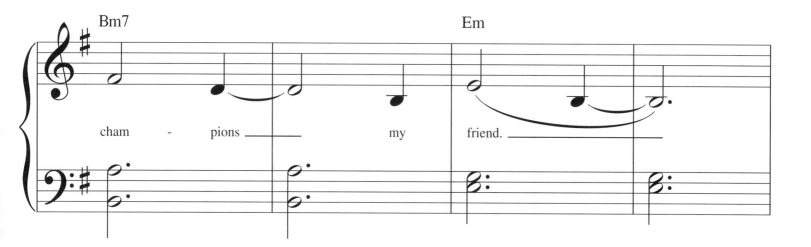

Bm7   Em

cham - pions ___ my friend. ___

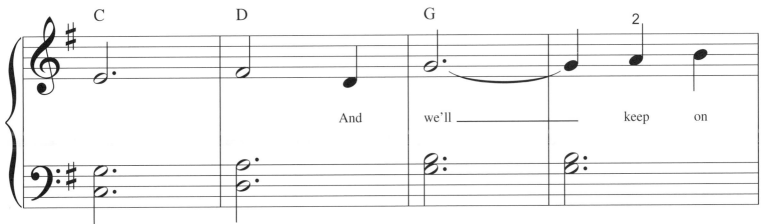

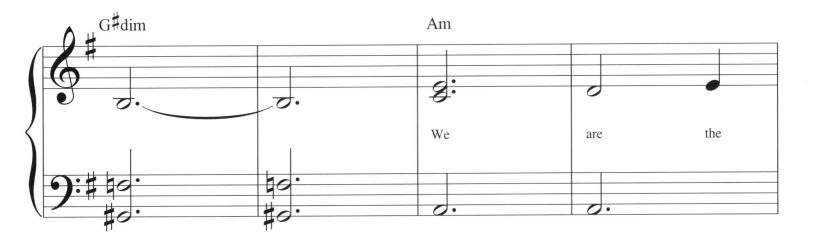

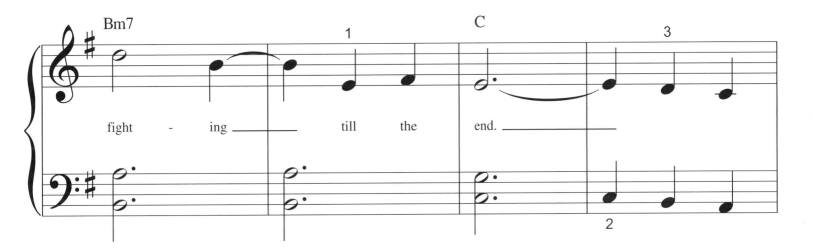

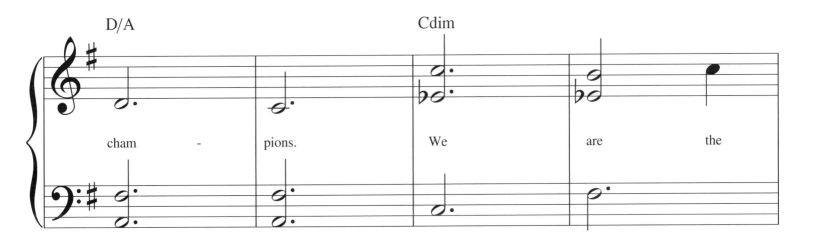

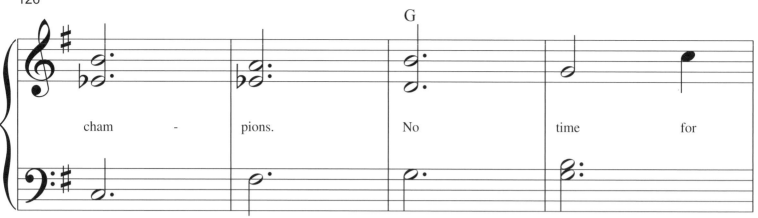

cham - pions. No time for

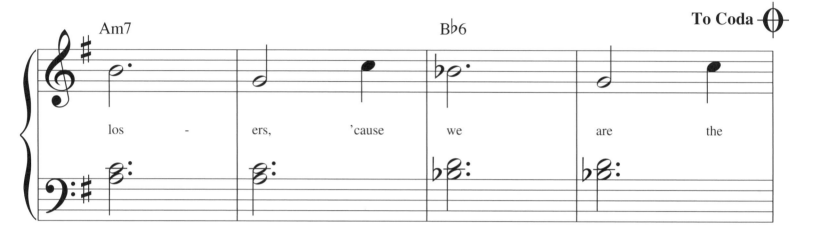

To Coda ⊕

los - ers, 'cause we are the

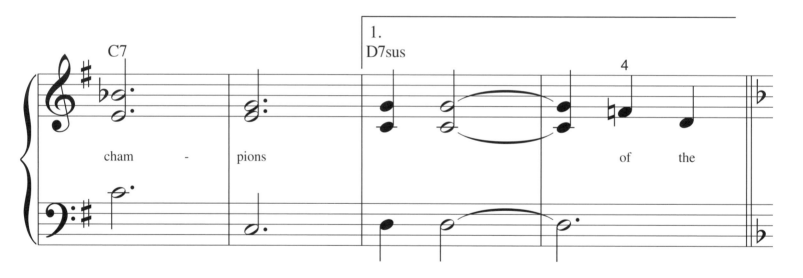

cham - pions of the

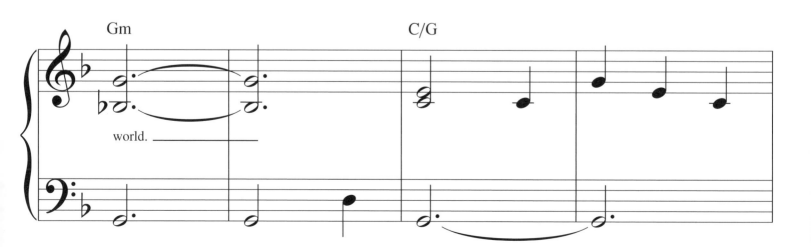

world. _____

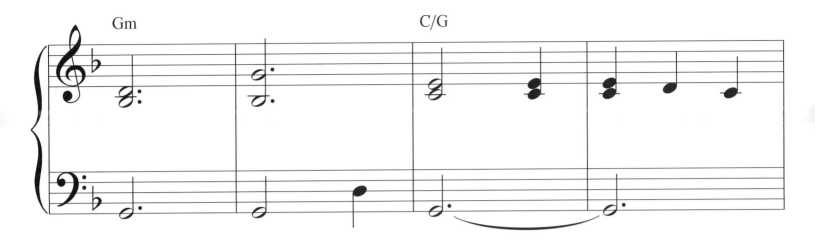

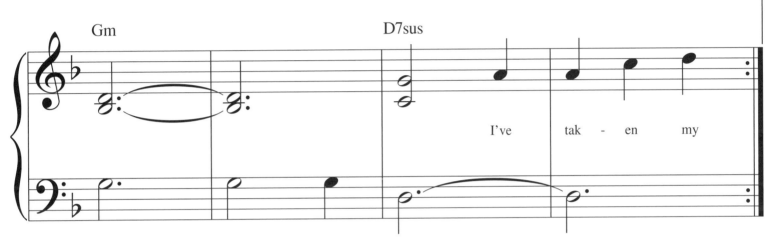

I've tak - en my

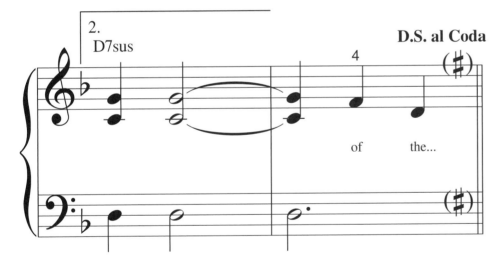

D.S. al Coda

of the...

CODA

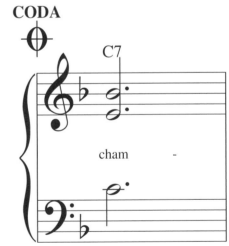

cham -

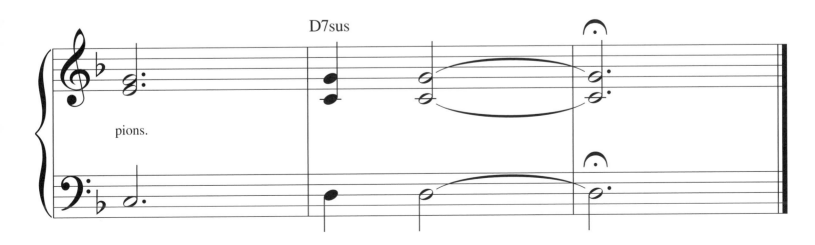

pions.

WHAT A WONDERFUL WORLD

Words and Music by GEORGE DAVID WEISS
and BOB THIELE

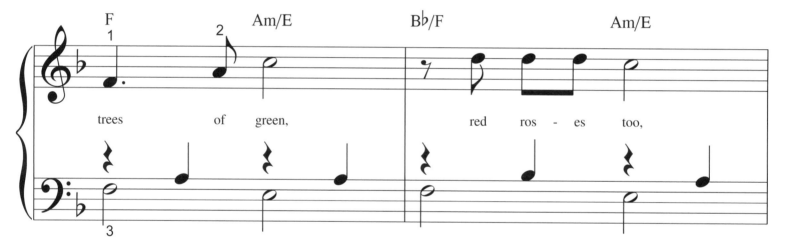

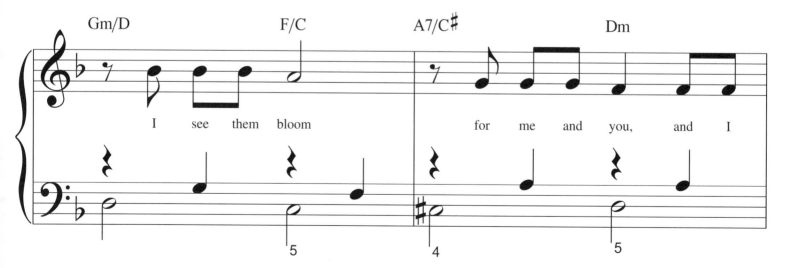

Copyright © 1967 by Range Road Music Inc., Quartet Music and Abilene Music, Inc.
Copyright Renewed
All Rights for Quartet Music Administered by BUG Music, Inc., a BMG Chrysalis company
International Copyright Secured   All Rights Reserved
Used by Permission

129

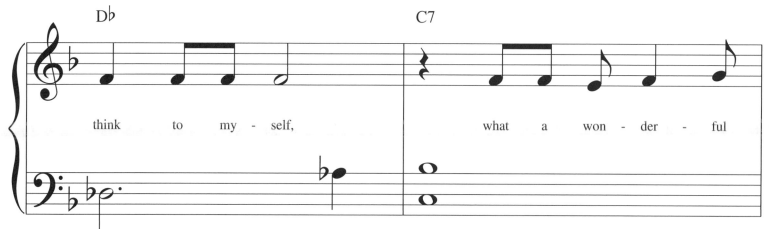

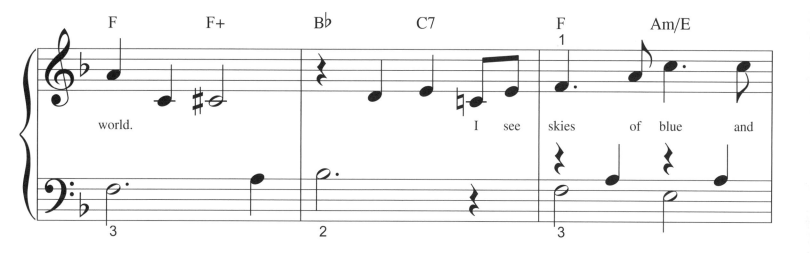

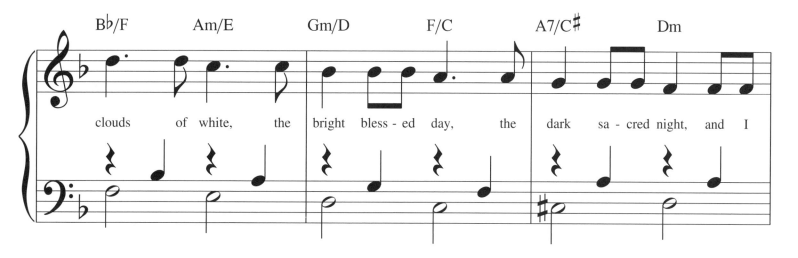

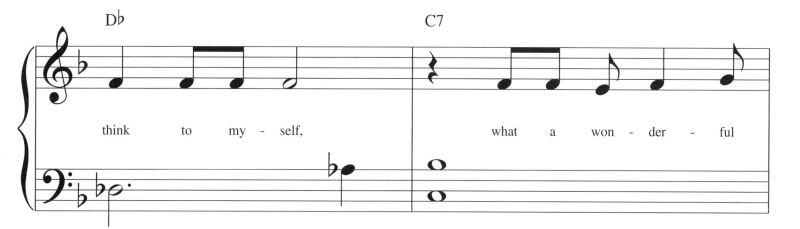

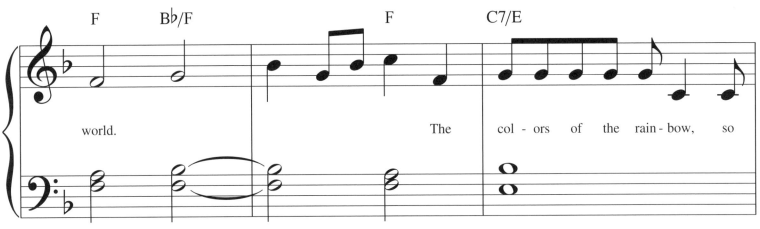

F   B♭/F   F   C7/E

world.   The   col - ors   of   the   rain - bow,   so

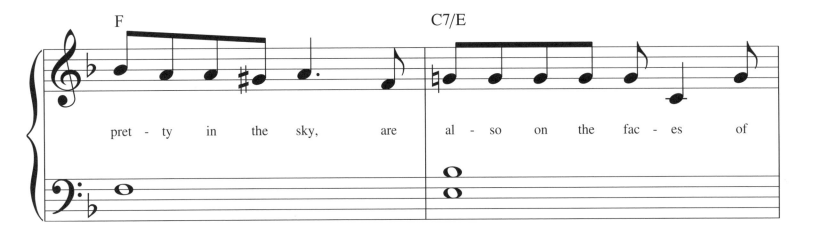

F   C7/E

pret - ty   in   the   sky,   are   al - so   on   the   fac - es   of

F   Dm   C/E

peo - ple   go - in'   by.   I   see   friends   shak - in'   hands,   say - in',

Dm/F   C/G   Dm/F   F♯dim   Gm   F♯dim   C

"How   do   you   do?"   They're real - ly   say - in',   "I   love   you."   I   hear

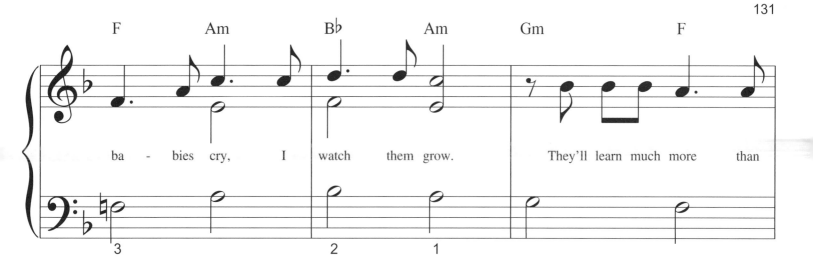

ba - bies cry, I watch them grow. They'll learn much more than

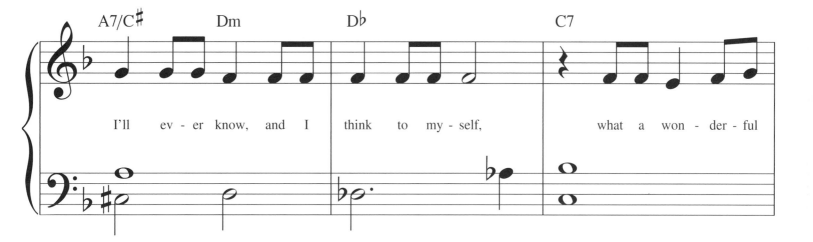

I'll ev - er know, and I think to my - self, what a won - der - ful

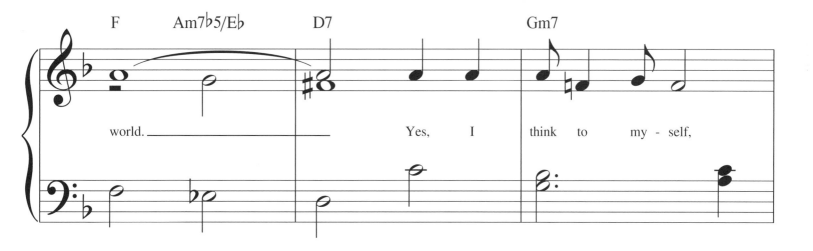

world. _____ Yes, I think to my - self,

what a won - der - ful world. *rit.*

WHAT THE WORLD NEEDS NOW IS LOVE

Lyric by HAL DAVID
Music by BURT BACHARACH

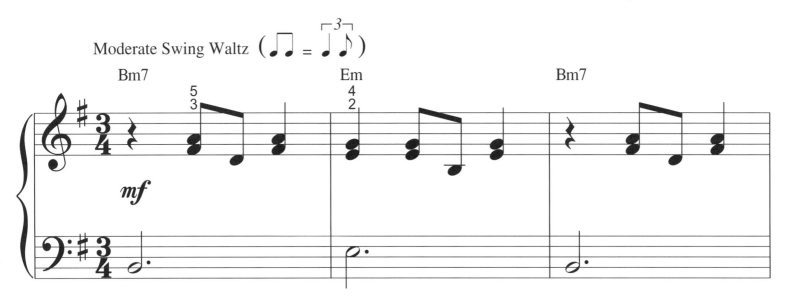

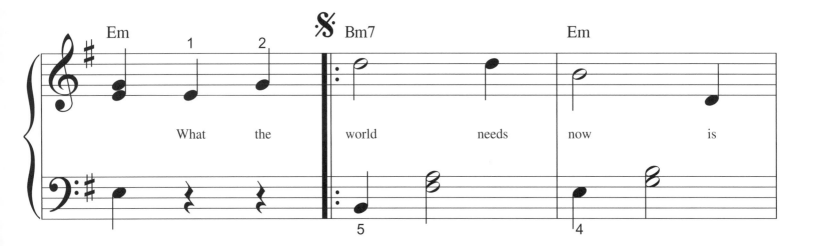

What the world needs now is

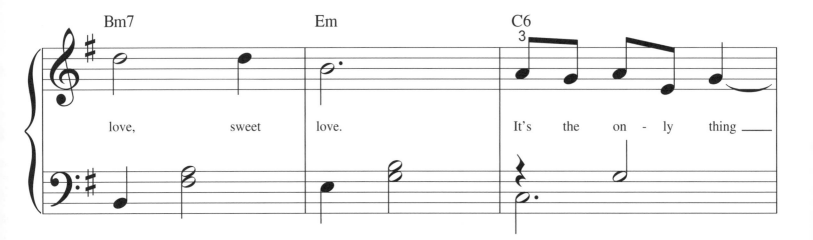

love, sweet love. It's the on-ly thing

Copyright © 1965 (Renewed) Casa David and New Hidden Valley Music
International Copyright Secured   All Rights Reserved

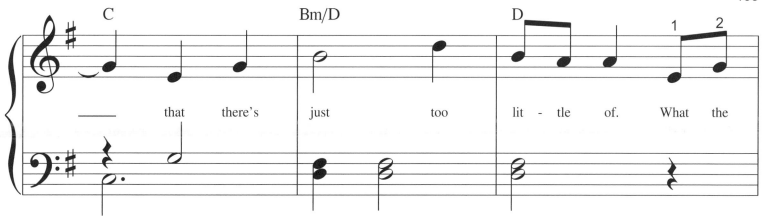

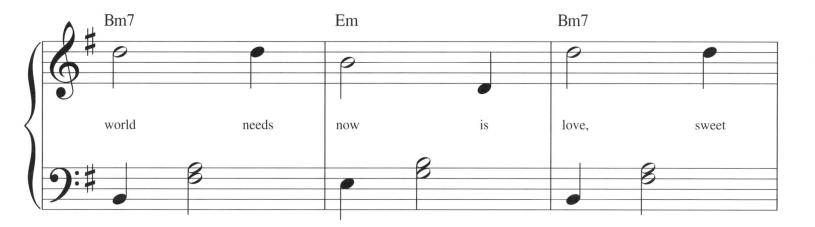

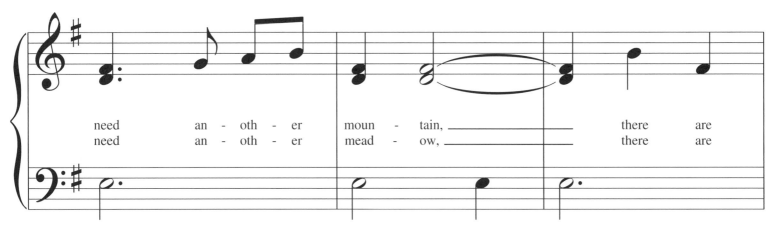

need   an - oth - er   moun - tain, _____   there   are
need   an - oth - er   mead - ow, _____   there   are

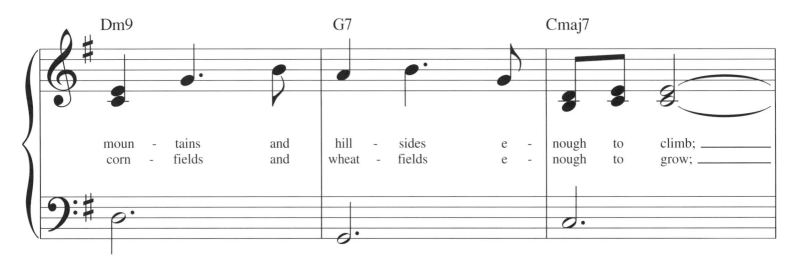

Dm9   G7   Cmaj7

moun - tains   and   hill - sides   e - nough   to   climb; _____
corn - fields   and   wheat - fields   e - nough   to   grow; _____

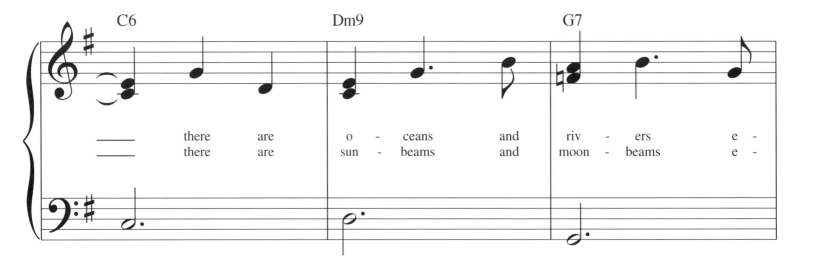

C6   Dm9   G7

_____   there   are   o - ceans   and   riv - ers   e -
_____   there   are   sun - beams   and   moon - beams   e -

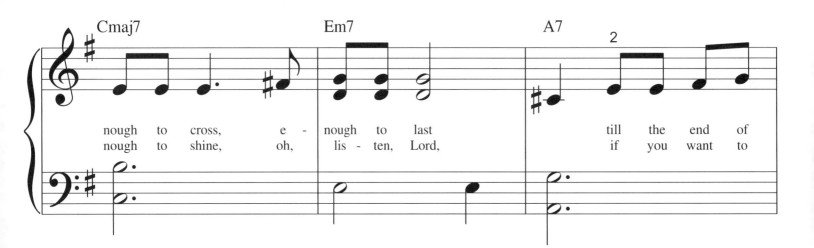

Cmaj7   Em7   A7   2

nough   to   cross,   e - nough   to   last   till   the   end   of
nough   to   shine,   oh,   lis - ten,   Lord,   if   you   want   to

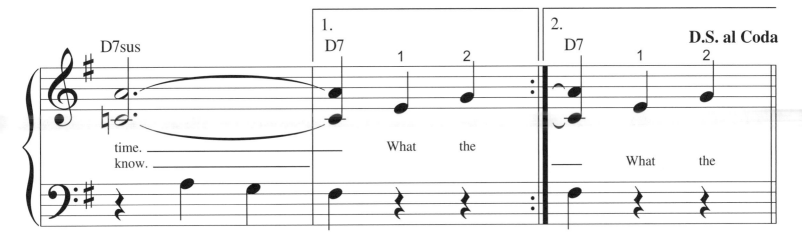

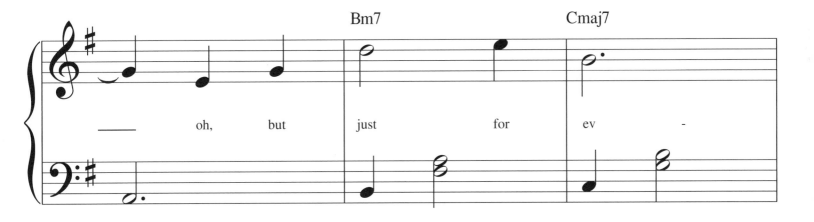

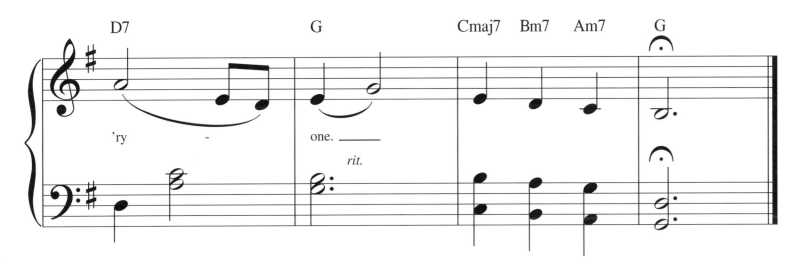

THE WIND BENEATH MY WINGS

Words and Music by LARRY HENLEY
and JEFF SILBAR

Slowly flowing, in 2

It must have been cold _____ there in my
I was the one _____ with all the
It might have ap - peared _____ to go un -

shad - ow, _____
glo - ry, _____
no - ticed, _____

to nev - er have sun -
while you were the one _____
but I've got it all _____

- light on your face.
with all the strength,
here in my heart.

© 1982 WARNER HOUSE OF MUSIC and WB GOLD MUSIC CORP.
All Rights Reserved   Used by Permission

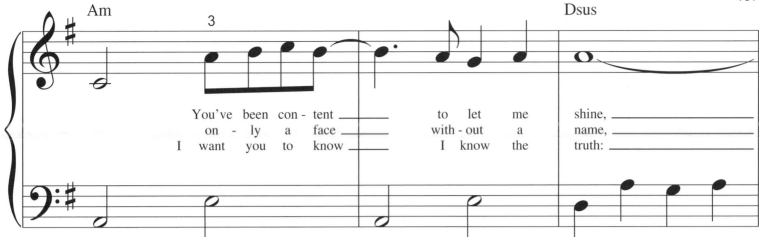

Am ... Dsus

You've been con - tent ____ to let me shine, ____
on - ly a face ____ with - out a name, ____
I want you to know ____ I know the truth: ____

D ... Am

you al - ways walked ____ the step be -
I nev - er once ____ heard you com -
I would be noth ____ ing with - out

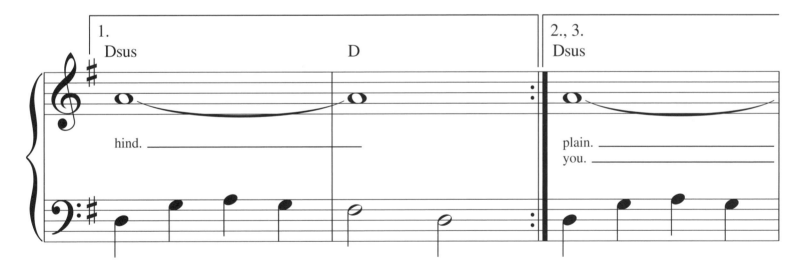

1. Dsus ... D | 2., 3. Dsus

hind. ____
plain. ____
you. ____

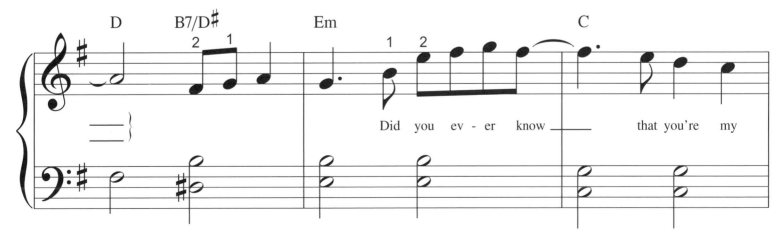

D B7/D# Em C

Did you ev - er know ____ that you're my

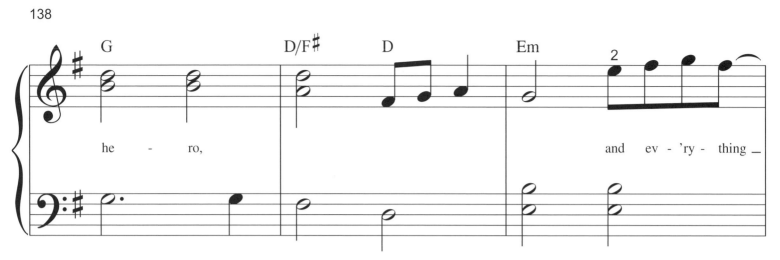

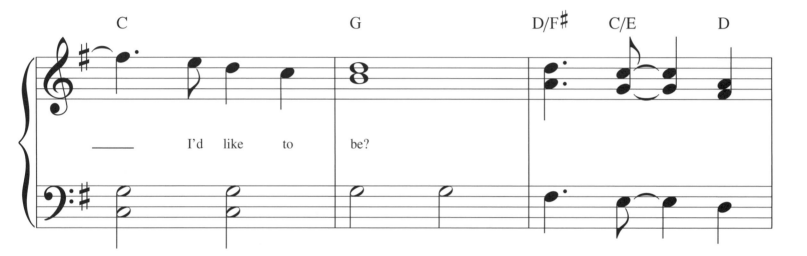

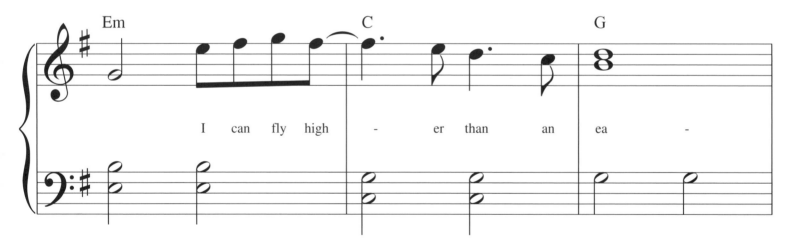

wings.

D.S. al Coda
(take 2nd ending)

CODA

wings.

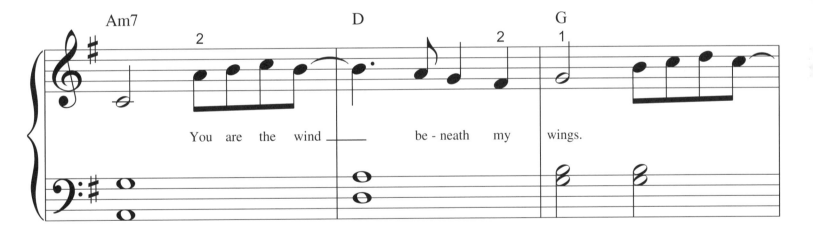

You are the wind be - neath my wings.

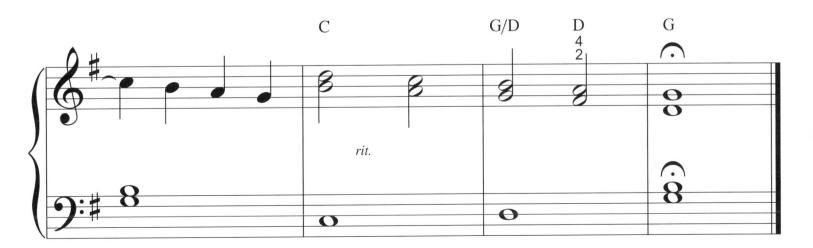

rit.

YOU RAISE ME UP

Words and Music by BRENDAN GRAHAM
and ROLF LOVLAND

Moderately slow

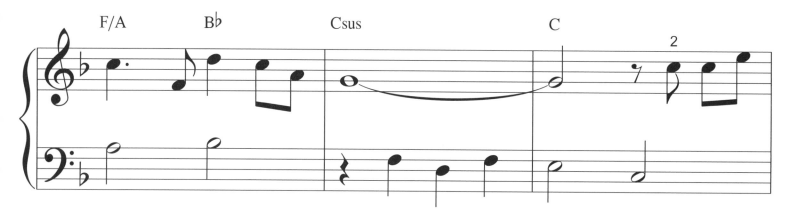

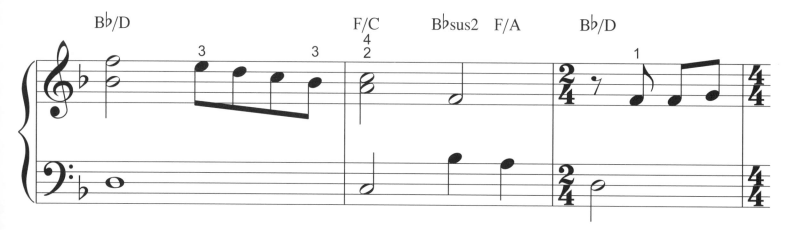

Copyright © 2002 by Peermusic (UK) Ltd. and Universal Music Publishing, A Division of Universal Music AS
All Rights for Peermusic (UK) Ltd. in the United States Controlled and Administered by Peermusic III, Ltd.
All Rights for Universal Music Publishing, A Division of Universal Music AS in the United States and Canada Controlled and Administered by
Universal - PolyGram International Publishing, Inc. (Publishing) and Alfred Music (Print)
International Copyright Secured   All Rights Reserved

When I am down and oh, my soul so wea - ry, when trou - bles

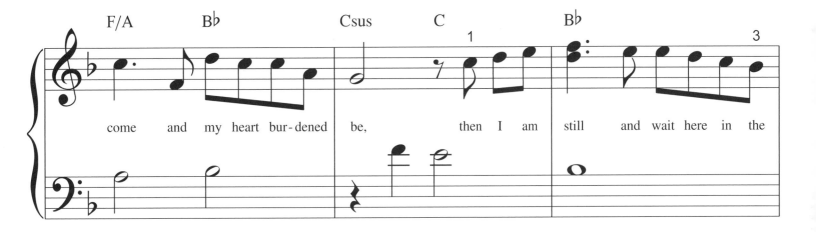

come and my heart bur - dened be, then I am still and wait here in the

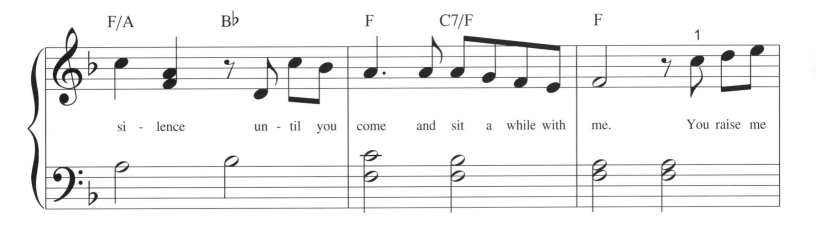

si - lence un - til you come and sit a while with me. You raise me

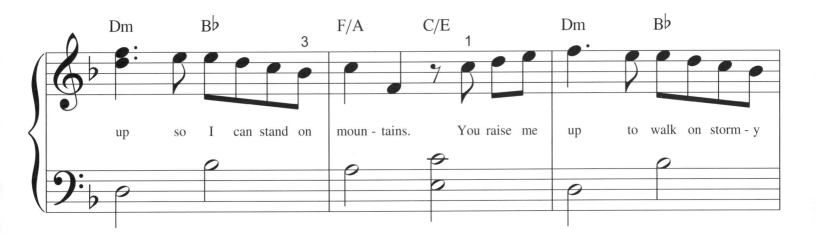

up so I can stand on moun - tains. You raise me up to walk on storm - y

142

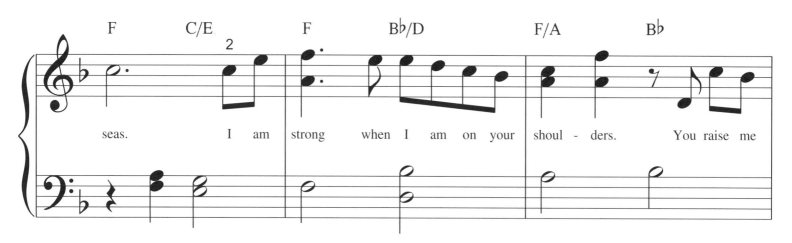

seas.   I am   strong   when I am on your   shoul - ders.   You raise me

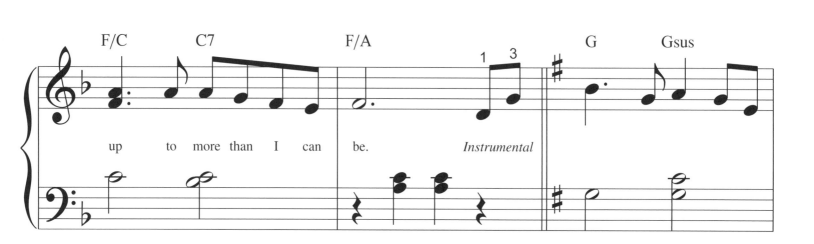

up   to more than I can   be.   *Instrumental*

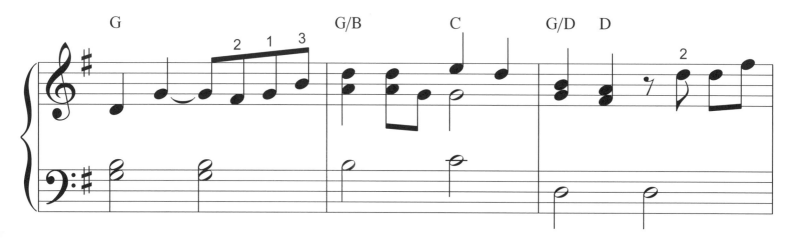

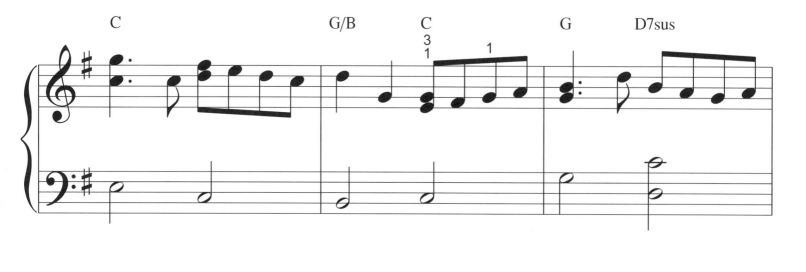

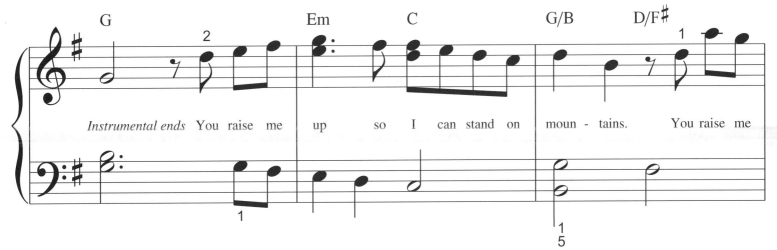

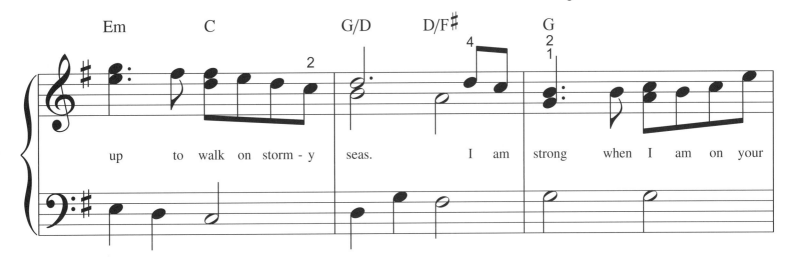

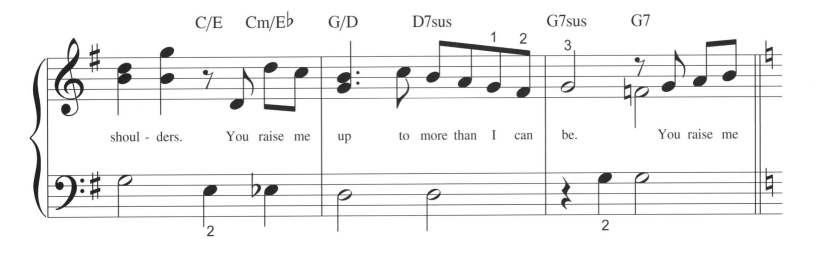

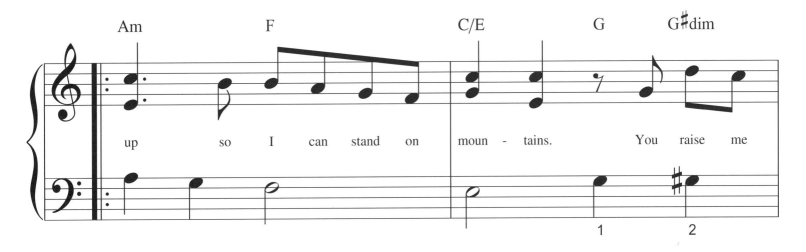

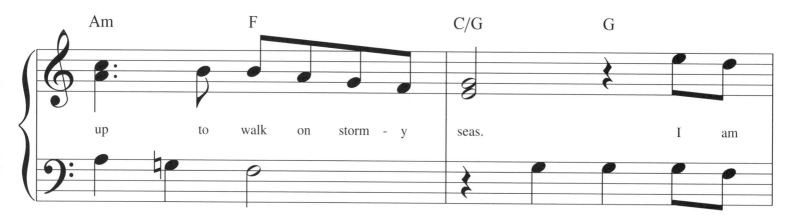

up   to walk   on storm - y   seas.   I am

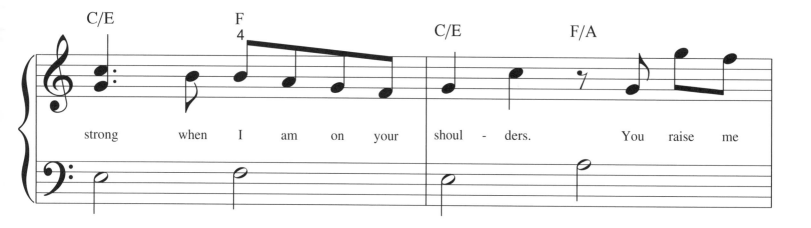

strong   when I am on your   shoul - ders.   You   raise me

up   to more than I can   be.   You raise me   up   to

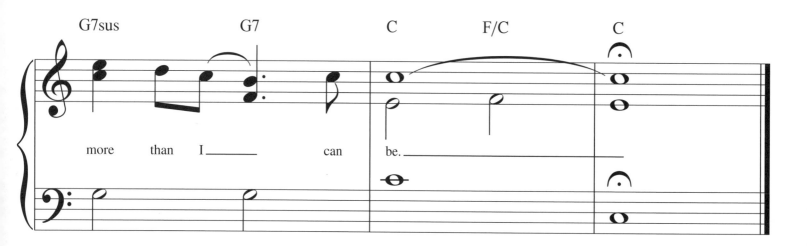

more   than   I _____   can   be. _____